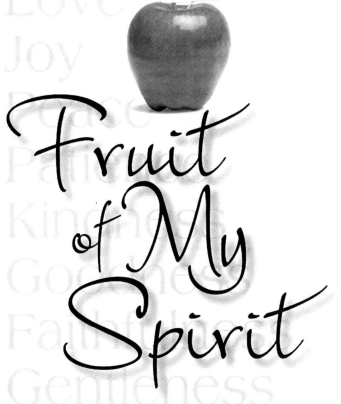

Love
Joy
Peace
Patience
Kindness
Goodness
Faithfulness
Gentleness
Self-Control

Fruit of My Spirit

Reframing Life in God's Grace

DEANNA NOWADNICK

Rhododendron
Books
Monroe, Washington

Fruit of My Spirit

Reframing Life in God's Grace

Although the author and publisher have made every effort to ensure the accuracy and completeness of information contained in this book, we assume no responsibility for errors, inaccuracies, omissions, or any inconsistency herein. Any slighting of people, places, or organizations is unintentional. Some names have been changed to protect privacy.

Scripture taken from the HOLY BIBLE, NEW INTERNATIONAL VERSION® NIV®. Copyright © 1973, 1978, 1984 by International Bible Society. Used by permission of Zondervan Publishing House. All rights reserved.

First printing 2012

ISBN 978-0-9835897-2-3
Library of Congress Control Number: 2011919373

ATTENTION CORPORATIONS, UNIVERSITIES, COLLEGES, AND PROFESSIONAL ORGANIZATIONS: Quantity discounts are available on bulk purchases of this book for educational and gift purposes, or as premiums for increasing magazine subscriptions or renewals. Special books or book excerpts can also be created to fit specific needs. For information, please contact Rhododendron Books, P.O. Box 1586, Monroe, WA 98272; (206) 370-9278; www.rhododendronbooks.com.

Table of Contents

List of Photographs

To my mother and father,
who asked me to write a book.

Acknowledgments

As I enter the seventh inning stretch of this wonderful publishing project, I'm acutely aware of the team that has surrounded me from my first pitch many months ago. I am humbled by the love and friendship of so many in my life. I can't thank you enough for just being there.

My husband Kurt

This summer we celebrated our thirtieth anniversary, an occasion that needed two cards since one just wasn't enough. Actually there will never be enough words to express my love for you. Not a day goes by that I don't thank God for your love and friendship. You are without compare. Your story has been intimately connected with my own story, and I thank you for allowing me to share it with the world.

My sons Kyle and Kevin

You are my greatest joy! To have been your mother will forever remain my greatest role in this life. As you grew, I grew. As you became wiser, I became wiser. I started writing, because I wanted you to know how I met your father. In the process, I got to tell of our many blessings as a family. I also got to share a few lessons from life. It's what a mother does.

My brother David

We grew up together. I admire you in so many ways. You navigate this life with a quiet strength and a dignified conviction, especially admirable after surviving the antics of your sister. I treasure our time together. I love knowing what you think and how you see this world. For being so difficult for so long, may this book serve as my sincerest apology.

My friend Nancy

You cradled an early copy of an unfinished manuscript and encouraged me to keep writing. Over coffee you urged me to believe in myself and my story. Your words meant the world to me as I struggled to find my own words. That afternoon, as you touched the pages of a notebook, you touched my heart. You are a dear friend.

My pastor Robin

God has always surrounded me with pastoral wisdom and guidance. With you, I've learned to delight in the unknown and the unanswerable, to savor the biggest and the smallest, and to rest in the blessed assurance of my place in God's family and God's place in mine. I appreciate your friendship and support, and your wisdom and experience, as I've ventured forth as a writer.

My publishing team who made it all happen
Sue, Kate, Aletha, and Juanita

I could not have done it without you! May I repeat that? I could not have done it without you! This time I was cradling the unfinished manuscript, looking for encouragement and direction. Not only did you steer me through uncharted waters, but you protected my own voice in the process. I am delighted with the book. I am truly grateful for your time and attention to detail and for caring enough to help me be my best.

But the fruit of the Spirit is love, joy, peace, patience, kindness, goodness, faithfulness, gentleness and self-control. Against such things there is no law.

Galatians 5:22-23
—the Apostle Paul in his letter
to the people of Galatia

Preface

Reframing Life in God's Grace

Preface

I'm a mess. The highlights in my hair hide a pre-gray drab. One hip and one knee have been replaced and another knee should be. I'm overweight and under the illusion that I'm going to wake up one morning to a younger, skinnier self. On good days I whine and complain. On bad days I whine and complain more. I'm impatient whenever life has the audacity to thwart my plans. I get frustrated whenever life presents a detour or a hurdle. At one point I planned to live to 125. When I remembered that the Bible says Moses only lived to 120, I decided on 119. I can't imagine God needing me around longer than Moses.

Life has its challenges. Life is a challenge. I know my existence is about more than this body. I know it's not about gray hair, failing body parts, and excess pounds. I know the important stuff's on the inside, but honestly, I'm not so sure that the inside stuff's any prettier. Perhaps I've been expecting God to act as my own fairy godmother, ready to pop into the scene any moment now with a twinkle in His eye and a wand in His hand. I've been waiting to be tapped ever so gently on the forehead and magically transformed into a loving, joyous, peaceful, patient, kind, good, faithful, gentle, self-controlled delight in His life, adorned in a nice white ensemble, cute shoes, and fresh nail polish. In thinking that, I've not only trivialized God's love and forgiveness, but I've missed the magnitude of His mercy that's been shared with me over and over again. I've overlooked the fruit of His Holy Spirit that's already a part of my own spirit in all that I do and all that I am.

So now what? Filled with His Holy Spirit, do I step back from life as I've known it? Do I need to tiptoe around the messiness of each day, avoiding the dirt and grime of my daily existence? If not wearing a white ensemble, something off-white? With His fruit, will I have this new aura about me that parts the seas and calms the storm within?

From an early age, I've been told that I am a child of God. I was brought up in the church. I went to Sunday School and Vacation Bible School. I attended youth group. In high school and college I worked part-time in the church office. I was active as a child, as a young person, and as an adult. That being said, I've still wondered at times about my place in God's family and God's place in mine. When the lights are turned out and I've left the church building, is there really a spot in God's heart for a defiant child? In His divine plans for a self-centered teenager? In His family for an adult who gets tired, impatient, frustrated, and distracted? Just having to ask tells me that I've truly failed to grasp the enormity of God's love and mercy. And today, I stumble through life trying to understand a gift that has no measure, picking myself up, only to trip on the very next hurdle. Bumped and bruised I've failed to see God's incredible ability to make the best out of the worst, the most out of the least, using forgotten moments, selfish intentions, and regrettable mistakes all for His glory.

I think I have a pretty good understanding of God's gift of unmerited love and complete forgiveness intellectually. Like any good Sunday School student, I could put together a well-worded essay on the tenets of faith; my head's got it. But my heart's not so sure. I realize now that I've rested in my intellect without finding comfort for my soul. I've reacted to life with the frustrations of a child, the hurts of a teen, and the failings of an adult. I have buckled under the weight of God's law and found it harder and harder to stand tall in the light of His love and grace. I've let my own plans and ambitions trump God's will for me in my life. I've ignored His blessings, focusing instead on life's challenges, and let the what-ifs consume my thoughts and energy. And now wrongdoings and shortcomings, imperfections and transgressions have become stone tablets amounting to fifty-six pounds of excess weight.

So here's where I find myself: I'm sitting in church on Sunday morning. We've just sung a couple uplifting songs of welcome. Next is the Confession of Sins (for all those wrongdoings, shortcomings, imperfections, and transgressions):

Most merciful God, we confess that we are by nature sinful and unclean. We have sinned against You in thought, word, and deed, by what we have done and by what we have left undone. We have not loved You with our whole heart; we have not loved our neighbors as ourselves. We justly deserve Your present and eternal punishment. For the sake of Your Son, Jesus Christ, have mercy on us. Forgive us, renew us, and lead us, so that we may delight in Your will and walk in Your ways to the glory of Your holy name. Amen.

Some Sundays we're more blunt: "I, a poor miserable sinner, confess unto Thee that I am by nature sinful and unclean." And with those words, I'm left in a poor, miserable place with no room to hide behind the collective voice of the congregation. God has offered me errors and omissions insurance and I'm still opting to fight my own battles in court—day after day after day. I've not only returned His gift of forgiveness unopened, but I've left him waiting in the foyer of my life as I linger endlessly at the pity party for innumerable mistakes. God's patience has been undeniable and completely undeserved. He has waited when I couldn't be bothered, when I was determined to go it alone, when I had a "better" idea, an easier solution. As the failures amassed and life's struggles accumulated, He remained faithful, loving and caring for me, guiding and pushing me.

By focusing on the trials of this life, I've overlooked the forgiveness that comes immediately after my confession in the pew. I've missed the harvest that springs forth from seeds of grace. And in doing so, I've missed the fruit of God's Spirit described so eloquently in Paul's letter to the people of Galatia, a letter written in part to help new Christians who had lived under Old Testament law move forward in New Testament grace. He passionately encouraged them to live by the Spirit and to share in the fruit of the Spirit:

> *But the fruit of the Spirit is love, joy, peace, patience, kindness, goodness, faithfulness, gentleness and self-control. Against such there is no law.*
> *—Galatians 5:22–23*

With Paul's encouragement and God's blessing, I want to reframe my own life in God's love and grace. I want to take the memories, those pictures that have been hanging on the walls of my heart, and reframe them. I want to replace broken glass, bad matting, and damaged wood. Together with God, I want to redo each photo, this time concentrating on the beauty of each remembrance, this time surrounded by a frame of love and forgiveness. Through it all I want to focus on the hugeness of God's faithfulness. There won't be a tap on my forehead; there will be no magical moments. This is real life, not a cartoon recreation. God's holding my hand, not a wand. He's really there; He has been all along. He has loved me without hesitation every day, every moment, through the best and the worst. I've truly been a part of His most glorious plan and most wonderful purpose. The Divine Master has been using my life and my missteps in the creation of a beautiful masterpiece, a blessed work of art colored with love and hope, highlighted with mercy and joy, and signed by the Almighty Himself, my Lord, my Savior.

As I go forth with God, my efforts to reframe life's experiences are not just redecorating projects; they're an opportunity to look back and see His love and forgiveness, to recognize the fruit of His Holy Spirit in my life. More importantly, they're the chance to see a bigger purpose, something that's been easy to overlook. God created me in His image. I was blessed to be a blessing. God picked me for a special purpose—one that would require the talents and experiences of a middle-aged woman, someone who had known both joy and heartache, someone who had lived life to its fullest, yet also known the regret and sorrow of a wasted moment and a neglected opportunity. He wanted my strengths and my weaknesses, my quirks and my flaws, my loves, my passions, and even my ditziness.

I'm not a child of God because people told me so; I'm His child because He made me so. He has loved and cared for me without fail through the best of times and during the most trying. When the lights were turned out and I left the church building, He left with me. And as part of His family, my growth in Him brought forth the fruit of my own spirit, imperfect, a little blemished, but delicious, sealed in His grace, fruit that has been a part of all that I do and all that I am. And now I look back with patience and understanding and look ahead with hope and joy. More importantly, I pause in gratitude for a God who was willing to include me in His unique and blessed plans for yesterday, today, and tomorrow.

And so I pray:

May the God of hope fill me with all joy and peace as I trust in him,
so that I may overflow with hope by the power of the Holy Spirit. Amen.
                                                                    —Romans 13:13

With God, it can be so. Today I plan for the harvest by planting seeds of hope and promise, wisdom and insight. Together with my Lord and Savior, I look back at life's struggles with new eyes, recognizing the work of the Holy Spirit in ways never before imagined or acknowledged. Those battered frames really do surround pictures of inestimable worth.

So, as the old hymn proclaims, "This is my story, this is my song!"

Blessed Assurance
Words by Fanny J. Crosby
Music by Phoebe P. Knapp

Blessed assurance, Jesus is mine!
O what a foretaste of glory divine!
Heir of salvation, purchase of God,
Born of His Spirit, washed in His blood.
    This is my story, this is my song,
    Praising my Savior all the day long;
    This is my story, this is my song,
    Praising my Savior all the day long.

Perfect submission, all is at rest!
I in my Savior am happy and blest,
Watching and waiting, looking above,
Filled with his goodness, lost in His love.
    This is my story, this is my song,
    Praising my Savior all the day long;
    This is my story, this is my song,
    Praising my Savior all the day long.

Love
Meeting Kurt

Agape

Greek for Love
The inexplicable love of God

Chapter One

I MET KURT AS AN 18-YEAR-OLD FRESHMAN in college. Kurt had been recommended to me by older classmates who had seen him at a local establishment specializing in pitchers of beer and chicken drumettes, pool, air hockey, and darts. Jim's 21 21 was also known for its more lenient enforcement of the drinking age, helpful for football players during the off-season and the young ladies in their shadow who were not yet 21. After seeing Kurt and his buddies enjoying a pitcher and some pool, friends from my dorm returned with helpful, although slightly inebriated, advice for their love-starved floor mate whose criterion for a possible love interest was limited and hunger for prospects insatiable. They confirmed for me that Kurt had been a starter during the fall football season and suggested I give him some consideration. Needing no more than an upperclassman's drunken endorsement and a vision of a cutie in a football jersey, I promised to seek him out, forgetting for the moment that my referral was coming from the drama student who three months earlier had been sitting on the steps of the building emoting through swirls of cigar smoke as new freshmen moved in with the aid of startled moms and dads.

My goal to meet Kurt became a mission. Never having had a diary as a young girl, I decided this special adventure was worth the time and paper. I was so sure that meeting Kurt would be a momentous occasion and one worthy of reflection that I logged every chance sighting and hormonally charged thought and feeling. My daily observations continued without fail for weeks. I knew when he ate, when he went to class, when he studied. I knew his football friends and the people in his dorm.

Living in my own all-girl dorm, I had close friends and casual acquaintances on the lookout for me, never missing the opportunity to report on Kurt's daily adventures: "I think I saw Kurt on the second floor of the library in one of the study carrels." If Kurt was studying, I suddenly had things to do in the library. If Kurt was eating late, I could be found visiting with friends long into the dinner hour, waiting to spot him with a tray of institutional spaghetti. I thrived on the possibility of just seeing him walking into the room, sitting and eating, grabbing a second serving of whatever.

My quest to meet Kurt was really that superficial. Today I think it would have been described with another S word: stalking. I watched, observed, and dare I say, spied, journaling throughout. Upperclassmen had said Kurt was pretty cute and suddenly I was on a mission to meet him. His quiet confidence became intoxicating, his intensity bewildering yet captivating, and for the moment, he was totally oblivious to the intense scrutiny of one freshman who had him in focus morning, noon, and night. I had yet to hear him speak, I had yet to make eye contact with him, but I had meticulous documentation of daily sightings and my own emotional reactions.

Kurt and I finally met at a party during interim, a month-long break between the fall and spring semesters. During January, students took just one or two classes, providing us with an opportunity to tackle a particular area of study for a shorter, more intense period of time. It also gave us a month to partake in social gatherings on campus and off without the rigors of an ordinary class load of work and homework.

Early in the month friends and I headed to a nearby house of upperclassmen. In keeping with the football theme, they were actually the male portion of the school's cheerleading squad. I learned immediately upon entering that Kurt was part of the festivities. Fortified with the confidence of an alcoholic pre-function and weeks of intense scrutiny, I waltzed into the kitchen, interrupted whatever he might have been doing, smiled, and said, "Hi, I'm Deanna. I'm supposed to like you."

To say we began a special journey together hardly suffices. For me our introduction began a major overland trek as I waded through swamps of emotions and climbed mountains of insecurity. My thirty-second dance that night in the kitchen took me down a road with more drama than I could ever have imagined. My friends and roommates suffered through moments of pure bliss ("He called!") and devastating setbacks ("He was at Denny's with a girl from his dorm!").

Within minutes of meeting Kurt, I was totally smitten. I ached at the very thought of every encounter. I quickly overwhelmed him with an eighteen-year-old's angst and determination. For nine years Kurt and I dated, broke up, and got back together. To this day, I badger him about his timing, since many of our breakups occurred just prior to major holidays, like Christmas and birthdays. I still question whether he was coming up emotionally short or just short on cash for a gift.

Kurt's reluctance to commit before he was ready forced me to become independent, to find a career and opportunities separate from him. Rather than risk being found sitting home alone on a Friday night, I also plunged into an active social life that was more reflective of my ongoing annoyance with Kurt's determination than any real desire to make new friends.

After being married twenty-eight years, I gave Kurt an oversize valentine with a handwritten message, "You are the biggest and best part of my life." Had I known that first January that he would become the very love of my life, I'd like to think I could have dialed it down a notch or two, but I doubt it. With my journal set aside after that first introduction, my emotions went into an almost daily exercise of "he loves me—he loves me not." To think that this went on for nine years before we finally married, had to have exhausted an entire community of friends and relatives, especially my roommate Sheryl who counseled me through every slight and misunderstood intention.

And yet, thirty-seven years after that cringe-worthy introduction, I find myself in a marriage of sheer joy and happiness, in a relationship with my very best friend. I absolutely delight in my time with Kurt. When he's traveling, his calls are the highlight of my day. Our vacations together are a time of reconnection and relaxation, a time to enjoy a little solitude at the pool and dinner at our favorite restaurants, a time to catch up on the latest gossip and newest movie. And whether we're in the middle of an animated retelling of the day's events or savoring a quiet car ride, I'm happy—I'm just plain happy.

God took my superficial wants and desires and guided me to a man of character. In 1972 I saw a football player with the cutest butt. I saw blue eyes and curly hair. I saw a cool guy and had the audacity to believe that I was the cool girl missing in his life. And with that, God stepped in and dialed it down a notch, giving Kurt the strength to keep me at arm's length when necessary and within reach when the time was right. God walked beside us and between us from that first moment.

God took my raw, hormonally fueled emotions and shaped them into a heartfelt commitment to home and family. At our twenty-fifth wedding anniversary, we celebrated more than just years of marriage. At the time we shared an open letter to our sons Kyle and Kevin, in which we thanked God for the many blessings bestowed upon us, the most important being them. We reminded each young man that they were the very best part of our twenty-five years together as husband and wife, father and mother. As our sons, they had been our greatest joy.

I have been the benefactor of a "match made in heaven." God took a young woman with a beer in one hand and a cigarette in the other and placed her in a beautiful home of happiness and love. He took a "Harstad Hornie," as the residents of our dorm were not so affectionately called, and gave her the finest husband and most endearing family. Through it all, God remained faithful, when I needed Him and when I couldn't be bothered. He loved me at my silliest. He loved me when I cared only about finding the cutest guy and being the cutest girl. He forgave me when my priorities became entangled with selfish wants and desires.

Loving me as a daughter, God was there to mold and shape me. As His own dear child, I was blessed with a husband and two sons. Through their love and our love as a family, I learned to appreciate God's love for me personally. I began to understand a love that is divine, unconditional, and self-sacrificing, a "wide-open" love. I finally began to understand.

As a younger person I had tried and tried to grasp the breadth and depth of God's feelings for me, that poor, miserable sinner in the church pew. Remembering how I had challenged my own father and mother, how I had shunned their concern and support more times than I could count, I shuddered to think of my Father in heaven. I had seen the hurt and anger in my parents' eyes. I had heard the frustration in their voices. I had dared them to love me, and then I had taken that love and voted Democratic. I felt as out of step in God's family as I had in my own.

Through Kurt, Kyle, and Kevin I learned how God could love even me, especially me. Married to Kurt, I was blessed by God with a man who would love me just as I am, a man who would accept all my quirks and insecurities. He tolerates my "must haves" and "gotta dos." He listens when I'm disappointed and counsels when I'm uncertain. He suggests. He even understands that I will implode without chocolate.

My older son Kyle introduced me to the wonders of parenting. Holding him as a newborn forever changed me and my view of the world. I knew instantly that I loved him unconditionally. I knew he would fill me with genuine delight and moments of heartache, but I didn't care. As his mother, I would love and support him, nurture and care for him through any- and everything. And in return, God gave me a son who lives life in joy. He inspires me with his passion for whatever he's doing. Kyle is truly a man of character and motivation. And my love for him is unwavering. When he stumbles, I am there for him. When he has a question, I rely on my best advice. If he just needs to chat, I can't imagine anything more important.

Kevin, my younger son, is wise beyond his years. He has a depth of understanding that I value. He also has a wonderful ability to take life as it comes with grace and ease, which I also value. He is kind and caring. With his birth, I was again forever changed, as only he would change it. Again I experienced unconditional love. I got to celebrate their differences as I treasured my relationship with each of my sons. Expecting the capacity of my heart to divide between them, I was overwhelmed when it more than doubled in size.

Our love as a family made God's love real. God's feelings were no longer words on a page or simplified two-dimensional images. They were emotions I could see and touch as I walked with Kurt or talked with Kyle and Kevin. My office was next to Kevin's bedroom, and when he was younger, we had some of our best conversations through the wall, me at my desk and Kevin at his. Many nights I had nothing to do in my office, but not wanting to miss a question or a comment, I sat. Like the chats with his brother, nothing was more important. And like the chats with my sons, nothing is more important to my Father.

As days become weeks and weeks become years, it's easy to lose sight of God and His work in my life. It's easier to focus on the missed opportunities, the painful slights, and the unfulfilled list of prayer requests. Because my own relationship with God has had its ups and downs, it's easy to believe God's love for me has experienced similar cycles, that His support for me has come and gone, depending on the circumstances, but it's not true. God's love is inexplicable. It's an indescribable love that can take the worst of intentions and create the best results. It's a remarkable love that can take the good, the bad, and the ugly and transform it all into a glorious encounter, a divine moment, a beautiful life. As I think about the love I'm able to share with Kurt and my sons, I remember God's love for me, knowing that it is the fruit of His Spirit that I'm able to extend to each one of them.

God loves me just the way I am. God's love for me as His child is unconditional and unwavering. He's there for me—day and night. He's there, just waiting, just in case, knowing that a chat with me is more important than anything. He's there when I stumble. He's there when I need advice and counsel—and he doesn't care that I vote Democratic. God stood with me as a ditzy teenager and has continued to stand with me every day since.

I pray:

Thanks be to thee, my Lord Jesus Christ, for all the benefits Thou has given me, for all the pains and insults Thou hast borne for me. O most merciful Redeemer, Friend and Brother, may I know Thee more clearly, love Thee more dearly and follow Thee more nearly, day by day.

—St. Richard of Chichester

With God, it can be so. With the fruit of God's love, I am able to love. As His child, I am able to share His love with those around me. And as I look back on my life, I see beautiful remembrances of His love and care, all framed in the forgiveness of His Son.

Love Divine, All Loves Excelling
Words by Charles Wesley
Music by Rowland Hugh Prichard

Love divine, all loves excelling,
Joy of heaven, to earth come down!
Fix in us thy humble dwelling,
All thy faithful mercies crown.
Jesus, thou art all compassion,
Pure unbounded love thou art;
Visit us with thy salvation,
Enter every trembling heart.

Breathe, O breathe thy loving spirit
Into every troubled breath;
Let us all in thee inherit,
Let us find thy promised rest.
Take away the love of sinning;
Alpha and Omega be;
End of faith, as its beginning,
Set our hearts at liberty.

Come, almighty to deliver,
Let us all thy life receive;
Suddenly return, and never,
Never more thy temples leave.
Thee we would be always blessing,
Serve thee as thy hosts above,
Pray, and praise thee without ceasing,
Glory in thy precious love.

Finish then thy new creation,
Pure and spotless let us be;
Let us see thy great salvation
Perfectly restored in thee!
Changed from glory into glory,
Till in heaven we take our place,
Till we cast our crowns before thee,
Lost in wonder, love, and praise.

Amen

Self-Control
Learning to Speak

Egkrateia

Greek for Self-Control
Command or mastery over one's own behavior

Chapter Two

I STARTED KINDERGARTEN IN THE FALL of 1959, leaving a neighborhood of white picket fences for the excitement of school. Mom took me to my new classroom that first day. I was wearing a print dress with a collar trimmed in lace, saddle shoes, and white stockings. I held a new box of crayons and a special mat for naptime.

The schoolroom was located upstairs in a primary wing with the first and second graders. It was large by today's standards, lined with the tall windows found only in schools built decades earlier. Thirty-some desks were arranged in groups of four. Toys and puzzles lined the surrounding shelves; science displays covered the counters. We had a dollhouse as tall as I was, and I remember being absolutely mesmerized by it from the moment I first walked into the room. School was going to be wonderful.

For me kindergarten was a morning of finger painting, stories, music, and quiet time. Decades later the unforgettable smells are still with me: tempera paint, crayons, papier-mâché, paste. We learned to cut and glue; we swirled our hands and fingers through paint. We laughed together, sang together, and played together inside and out. We made new friends, discovered the magic of filmstrips, and found ways to share the dollhouse. School really was wonderful.

First grade was not so idyllic. Now we were learning real stuff, like reading and numbers. I spent an entire day at school with a teacher who expected me to pay attention and work—quietly. We were asked to cut and glue quietly, paint and color quietly. If I knew the answer to my teacher's question, I needed to raise my hand and wait quietly to be called upon. Before the first week was out, my optimism began to fade and I started to fear the challenges that loomed. This new routine didn't work for me. I had things to say and wanted badly to be heard. I didn't want to spend the next nine months watching day after day slip by—quietly. My carefree life as a verbal kindergartener had been erased in a few short days by the nonverbal intensity of first grade, and I soon found myself with a special place at the chalkboard. Here I stood with my nose in my teacher's hand-drawn circle, the consequence of my incessant chatter. I was never quite sure how time in front of the class with my nose pressed in chalk dust was expected to quiet me, but for whatever reason, that was her solution for my inability to keep still. For me, it meant a lot of time to mourn the joy of the previous year that had been left behind.

My first experience with a substitute teacher was worse. As any good sub would, she clearly stated her expectations regarding our reading and math assignments and the daily schedule, including recess and restroom breaks. Not wanting to be told what to do by this short-term fill-in, I listened carefully and then proceeded to ignore everything she asked of us. The day fell apart when we were given time to use the bathroom with the understanding that it would be our one and only break for the afternoon. She reminded us several times that we would not be allowed to leave the classroom after returning. I proceeded to walk down the hall with my class, strut into the bathroom, and prance right back out. Again she reminded me that this was my one chance to "go," but I said nothing and found my place in line. After walking back down the hall and reaching my desk, I sat down and with all the skill and determination of a defiant six-year-old, wet my pants. Without a word, I stood up and headed home as she jumped up from her desk, stunned. I was so pleased with myself as I left the room, and then I remembered the six-block walk ahead of me. I could only hope it would be long enough to come up with a plausible explanation for Mom.

In second grade, I was back in front of the class, this time getting the backs of my hands slapped with a ruler. My father loved to say that children were meant to be seen and not heard, a family motto that had evidently followed me to school. Unable to keep still, I suffered through the sting of embarrassment and humiliation as yet another teacher tried to reign in my mouth. All hope and promise for the new school year were gone as I stood in front of God and everyone for disciplinary action. It made no sense to me, but I said nothing—not to my friends, not to anyone, especially not to my parents. To schoolteachers, the very idea of breaking classroom rules was tantamount to breaking one of the Ten Commandments.

In third grade I stole a library book when I learned that it was going to be given to another student first. After being discovered and reprimanded by my teacher, I was sent home, again trying to explain the seemingly obvious: "But Mom, she never even asked me if I wanted to read it!"

In fifth grade I was sent home from day camp, because I refused to cooperate with my counselor. "But, Mom, she wouldn't listen to me!"

It took all of elementary school—seven teachers and seven grades, but I learned to behave. Before leaving, I actually became a good student, a model citizen. I was even on the school patrol my last year. Serving as a crossing guard, I found it ironic that by sixth grade I could be entrusted with the lives of small children on a four-lane thorough-fare, but I still couldn't be trusted to keep quiet when it was required of me. I just wanted to be able to speak—wherever I was, no matter what I was doing. Older and only a little wiser, I was sure that life didn't allow me a voice when I needed one, and I was straining at the restrictions, real and perceived, major and minor. In addition to spelling and arithmetic, I learned to internalize every possible emotion from anger and frustration to happiness and joy. I also became very self-centered, placing a greatly exaggerated value on too many unspoken thoughts and feelings.

By the time I was in junior high and then high school, my chafing at life became a full blown rebellion directed squarely at those closest to me: my mom and dad. I reacted with cynicism and animosity to their every effort at parenting. Mom and Dad were Depression-era babies who were trying to be responsible parents in the middle of the 1960s, people who turned on the evening news to reports of civil rights demonstrations, free love, and hallucinogenic drugs. They had seen their world go from black and white to color on the family's television set, an advancement in modern living that left them with nightly images of unrest and uncertainty in the streets and the horrors of jungle warfare in Southeast Asia. Much in their world seemed out of control, and sadly their daughter was now part of the chaos. Not wanting to appreciate their concerns, I responded to their advice and counsel with a glare, a sigh, a rude comment, or silence. Finally—silence. I had learned to shut up, at the very moment we most needed to speak.

My inability to communicate haunted my relationship with Mom and Dad for the rest of their lives. I destroyed any chance for harmony in our house by refusing to set aside pride and self-righteous indignation. From the outside our home looked absolutely beautiful, but the manicured lawns and carefully tended rhododendrons were in sharp contrast to the turmoil and heartache within. The pain left in my wake was truly excruciating and unwarranted.

At fifty-six I find myself responding to the stresses of life as a six-year old child with chalk all over her nose. It's fifty years later and I'm reacting to a long day with the same thoughts and internalized emotions. I deal with disappointment and misunderstandings like that small second grader dealt with the ruler—with anger and frustration. And as the feelings start to surface, as they come rushing forth, I fight back with a child's voice or a silent scream, turning to food to numb the spirit and quiet the soul. I have learned there is nothing that a carbohydrate can't soothe, that chocolate can't comfort. In his book, *The Good Listener*, James Sullivan describes our need to be heard as "a powerful, relentless hunger, that never diminishes and never goes away," and I would add, cannot be calmed with food.

It's easy to think I was just born at the wrong time in history, but I could easily have been standing before my class centuries earlier with coal dust on my nose. This is not about the need for a generational do-over. This is a story about the frustrations of my childhood continuing to haunt me years later, about the challenges of youth leaving an indelible imprint on my perceptions of life, remembrances that God is helping me to remat and reframe. God was with me throughout: He saw the turmoil; He understood the pain. At any given moment, He could have advised and counseled, but I chose to immerse myself in the hurts, pulling those closest to me into misery, heartache, and frustration.

But a faithful God loved and forgave. To the student who refused to shut up and listen, God provided a place to speak. He gave me the chance to teach in a public school. I got to be the teacher who couldn't be there for me. I graduated from college with a degree in English, planning to teach at a middle school or high school. I also had a Learning Disabilities endorsement, allowing me to teach students from kindergarten to the twelfth grade. With that endorsement, God put me into an elementary school and into a classroom of learning disabled students. There I was surrounded by children who had struggled in the regular program, failing time after time, children who had gotten lost in the masses. I got to listen to their stories, put Band-Aids on their hurts, and celebrate their accomplishments, however small. We talked and we talked and we talked. At that school, I found an unexpected contentment and a renewed sense of self, and in that room, with those children by my side, I learned to speak—in love and compassion.

To a daughter who insisted on stamping out her family's chance for peace and happiness, God gave the skills and abilities to mother two wonderful sons. He gave me Kyle and Kevin and relationships in which to share my own advice and counsel. It should come as no surprise that at times I spoke more than necessary, but when it was most important, I also listened. While in college, my younger son Kevin loved to give me grief about my constant contacts: "Mom, I just spoke with you last week." Today I continue to plague him and his brother with my usual greeting: "Hey, how's it going? What should I know?" Invariably the response is "Nothing, Mom," but with that question comes a mother's willingness to tackle the world's problems, someone who remains available to them anytime anyplace, and someone who loves them just as they are—imperfect sons of an imperfect mother. I may be delightfully annoying, but I am also wonderfully loving. The love of God's Holy Spirit has become the love of my own spirit, a love that God has helped me to share with two young men.

God didn't leave me broken and dispirited. He picked me up, cared for my own hurts with love and understanding, and used life to reassure me that it was going to be all right. He erased the circle from the chalkboard and allowed me to start anew. He helped me learn to control my emotions. He gave me a voice and a place to be heard. He calmed the storm within. The fury became tact. The frustrations became empathy. The misunderstandings became renewed efforts to listen and appreciate. God used my self-important view of life and shaped it into the confidence to believe in my skills and abilities, all God-given. He showed me opportunities to teach and lead in my work and within His church. He gave me interesting and unique ways in which to bring His people together.

God also helped me become the parent I refused to let my own parents be. I will forever regret that my wisdom and experience came at their expense. After living with the worst, they never got to enjoy the fruit of God's Spirit as it became the fruit of my own. God's forgiveness allowed me to step out of my brokenness and into the newness of another day. My parents were beyond reproach and I pray that God has shared that with them. As part of His family, He loved and cared for us all.

Looking back, my lessons in self-discipline are a remarkable picture with a wonderful new frame of love and forgiveness. To my Father in Heaven, I pray:

I thank You, O Lord, for giving me strength, Christ Jesus our Lord, because You judged me faithful, appointing me to Your service, though formerly I was a blasphemer, persecutor, and insolent opponent. But I received mercy because I had acted ignorantly in unbelief, and Your grace overflowed for me with the faith and love that are in Christ Jesus. The saying is trustworthy and deserving of full acceptance, that Christ Jesus came into the world to save sinners, of whom I am the foremost. But I received mercy for this reason, that in me, as the foremost, Jesus Christ might display His perfect patience as an example to those who were to believe in Him for eternal life. To You, Lord, the King of ages, immortal, invisible, the only God, be honor and glory forever and ever. Amen.

—based on 1 Timothy 1:12–17

With God, it can be so.

I recently learned that the King James Bible defines self-control's opposite as "incontinence." Who could have guessed! I was also given that book titled *The Good Listener*. Who could have known!

For this very reason, make every effort to supplement your faith with virtue, and virtue with knowledge, and knowledge with self-control and self-control with steadfastness, and steadfastness with godliness, and godliness with brotherly affection, and brotherly affection with love. For if these qualities are yours and are increasing, they keep you from being ineffective or unfruitful in the knowledge of our Lord Jesus Christ.

—2 Peter 1:5–8

Immortal, Invisible, God Only Wise
Words by Walter C. Smith
Music by John Roberts

Immortal, invisible, God only wise,
In light inaccessible hid from our eyes,
Most blessèd, most glorious, the Ancient of Days,
Almighty, victorious, Thy great Name we praise.

Unresting, unhasting, and silent as light,
Nor wanting, nor wasting, Thou rulest in might;
Thy justice, like mountains, high soaring above
Thy clouds, which are fountains of goodness and love.

To all, life Thou givest, to both great and small;
In all life Thou livest, the true life of all;
We blossom and flourish as leaves on the tree,
And wither and perish—but naught changeth Thee.

Great Father of glory, pure Father of light,
Thine angels adore Thee, all veiling their sight;
But of all Thy rich graces this grace, Lord, impart
Take the veil from our faces, the vile from our heart.

All laud we would render; O help us to see
'Tis only the splendor of light hideth Thee,
And so let Thy glory, Almighty, impart,
Through Christ in His story, Thy Christ to the heart.

Peace
Camping

Eirene

Greek for Peace
Tranquility, a state of rest

Chapter Three

I HATED CAMPING AS A CHILD and as a young person and had I gone camping as an adult, I would have hated it then, too. My outdoor experiences were commensurate with torture, a reflection that is only slightly exaggerated. I just never understood the joy of sitting on a log for hours on end with my hair smelling of smoke from a campfire. For me, it was either hot and sticky or cold and damp. Sometimes it was hotter and stickier; sometimes it was colder and damper. Bathrooms smelled of too much industrial-strength cleanser or worse, no cleanser at all. If God had meant for me and all of humankind to live in the trees surely He would have put us there....

With my graduation from Blue Birds in the second grade, I became a Camp Fire girl. In a new uniform, I got to attend weekly meetings filled with arts and crafts, snacks, and games. Our motto was "Wo-He-Lo," short for work, health and love, not exactly *Eat, Pray, Love*, but then we were only in grade school.

Life as a Camp Fire girl meant special projects and honor beads that became part of our ceremonial vests and gowns. It also meant camping. Since we were *Camp Fire* girls, camping was obviously going to be part of the repertoire. This made sense to me theoretically, but I chose to ignore the obvious and began to dread what lay ahead. So far we were just hanging out together, enjoying cocoa and s'mores around a backyard barbeque, but I knew that one day soon we were actually going to be venturing out with tents and sleeping bags.

As school ended each June and summer vacation began, the camping situation intensified, going from an overnight stay in someone's backyard to three-day getaways in the forest with hikes and dirt and bugs and distress. By fifth grade, it was time for the real thing—*camp*, a week in a canvas shelter under the trees at the official Camp Fire Girls campground on the shores of the Puget Sound. As everyone in the group anxiously awaited the day, I waited anxiously.

My seven days at camp started out tolerably with time for more arts and crafts, group activities and games, old friends and new. They were also filled with nighttime treks to the bathroom, mosquito bites, and overly long walks everywhere—to the dining hall, to the beach, to the tent. My hair got greasier by the day, my arms and legs smelled of insect repellent, and my stomach craved chocolate in any form, in any amount.

As the week progressed, preparations were made for a two-day canoe trip, an overnight saltwater adventure to a neighboring beach. On the big day, we filled canoes with food, sleeping bags, and cooking utensils and took off, some kneeling against the seats, others against the crossbeam, half of us paddling on one side, half on the other. It's hard to remember whether the trip was forty-five minutes or forty-five hours; it felt like the latter. It was probably just two or three hours, but that was two or three hours more than I would ever need again—and then I remembered that there would be a return trip the following day.

After arriving at our destination, we set about preparing the camp, parking our canoes upside down to dry over logs on the beach. Our arrival meant we were now without the benefit of a tent or access to a bathroom, a situation I would have passed on had anyone asked. That night we cooked dinner on our buddy burners, all to varying stages of doneness and edibility. After making a valiant attempt to clean dishes with water one degree above freezing, we joined together around the campfire for s'mores (finally) and "Kumbaya" (naturally). Little did we know that the elements would soon do more for our togetherness than an African spiritual.

Just minutes after midnight, the first sounds of thunder could be heard across the water. Moments later lightning flashed. With sleeping bags nestled between logs on the beach, we quickly scurried to the perceived safety of the boats as the storm raced across the sound. Crouched under *metal* canoes, we waited hours for the thunder and lightning to pass. We were cold and wet and miserable, but fortunately, not electrocuted.

By morning the storm was over, but I was optimistic about little else. I was soaked through to my skin and everything with me was equally saturated—food, gear, and my new sleeping bag. I didn't need breakfast; I needed to go home, and all I could think about was the three-hour paddle ahead.

I was soon pleading with my parents to be done with Camp Fire Girls, but to no avail: "You'll miss all your friends!" Honestly, the friendships I had at that moment in time were not worth the possibility of dying under a metal canoe in an electrical storm. Not one to give in easily, I continued to whine before and after every activity. Two years later, two long years later, Mom and Dad finally relented and my days as a Camp Fire girl were history. And my days as a camper were done—forever!

Today I don't camp—don't want to camp, don't need to camp. Our family goes to Crescent Bar, a resort area between Wenatchee and Quincy on the bend of the Columbia River. Skipping any form of canvas accommodations, we rent condos, one for the parents and one for the boys and friends who might come along. Together we relax, Mom at the pool with her coffee drink, the boys in the boat with Dad wakeboarding and skiing. Our rooms come with a dishwasher, garbage disposal, washer and dryer, shower, and queen-size bed. We have sheets and blankets, plates and silverware. We cook on a stove (sometimes) or eat out (often). We do not camp. On our way, we pass campgrounds, but we never stop—ever.

During this week away each summer I find rest and relaxation. Kurt, Kyle, Kevin, and I settle into a routine of twice-daily ski runs, afternoon naps, and dinners at our favorite local establishments, invariably including a birthday celebration for my son and his mother.

I was fortunate to be born when I was. God in His infinite wisdom made me a baby boomer, not part of the Westward Expansion. I've had visions of being abandoned on the plains, no canvas shelter, no chocolate, watching the last of the wagon train fade into the distance, all because I couldn't embrace anything about outdoor living. My whining would have threatened the very livelihood of the determined pioneers and forced them to make the not-so-difficult decision to leave me and my bedroll at the side of the trail.

But then God knows that about me. God knows everything about me: how I have to have the same nail polish on my fingers and toes, how I have to wear mascara to get the mail, how I hate to sweat, how I hated camping. In His image He made me, and against the backdrop of all humanity He made me unique and uniquely His. God knew I would try His patience and the patience of my family, teachers, and camp counselors. God knew He would have to pound out character flaws and recall my attitude. God knew I would be a piece of work.

And to this cellular mass of sin and doubt, God promised a different kind of peace, not the calm that comes after an electrical storm or the rest that comes poolside, but the peace given to me by His Son:

Peace I leave with you; my peace I give you. I do not give to you as the world gives. Do not let your hearts be troubled and do not be afraid.
—John 14:27

It is His peace that I would need in my heart. Huddled under a canoe as a young camper, I wanted refuge from the storm. Years later I wanted a well-earned vacation in the sun. To that temporary quiet, God would add a real peace, a peace not of this world, but an eternal peace.

For as long as I can remember, I've been hungry. Upon waking in the morning, I am starving. After the biggest meal, I crave another dessert. If I could, I would eat 24/7—and still want more. In high school I began a terrible struggle with an eating disorder, a shameful time that further separated me from God and His love and grace. I tried and I tried with bite after bite to find peace, to calm the storm within and quiet my raging thoughts and emotions. What started as a temporary reprieve from the stress of the day became a forty-year battle plan for dealing with life's ups and downs. For all those years I used food to celebrate and comfort.

When I started writing, I decided to stop dieting. I just couldn't ask God to go with me on this journey, only to hang onto food after asking for His hand. At the time I could imagine nothing more fearful, but I'd run out of energy and had no more strength to fight with myself. My heartfelt prayer was nothing more than, "Please, God." I didn't even have the words to know what to ask for. All I could repeat was, "Please, God."

For several weeks I ate any- and everything. I went back to the bakery and got my favorite almond brioche. I baked an apple cake—and had it for dinner one night and lunch the next day. I ate pasta, drank Pepsi, and enjoyed dinner with my son. God sat with me every day at every meal. He provided nourishment for my body and comfort for my soul. And for the first time ever, I left the table full—and at peace. When I finally gave up and gave in, God was able to give me His gift of peace. God took my painful past and granted me His complete forgiveness. God turned my focus from the comforts of this world to real comfort—peace in Him. God took my fear and replaced it with the courage to let go and let Him.

My struggles aren't over. I still have days that fall apart even with the best of intentions and the most fervent prayers. I'm not perfect, but I do have a new forty-year plan, God's plan.

God continues to bless me with weeks at Crescent Bar and holiday travels to the sun, family time that I treasure, especially as the boys get older. He also continues to bless me as part of His family. God chose me to be His own. He sacrificed His one and only Son that I might have life forever and ever—with Him. He gave me His Holy Spirit that I might bear fruit, His peace.

To my God, I pray:

Lord, make me an instrument of Your peace. Where there is hatred, let me sow love; where there is injury, pardon; where there is doubt, faith; where there is despair, hope; where there is darkness light; where there is sadness, joy.

—*St. Francis of Assisi*

With God, it can be so.

Built on the Rock
Words by Nikolai Fredrik Severin Grundtvig, translated by Carl Doving
Music by Ludvig M. Lindeman

Built on the Rock the Church shall stand
Even when steeples are falling.
Crumbled have spires in ev'ry land;
Bells still are chiming and calling,
Calling the young and old to rest,
But above all the souls distressed,
Longing for rest everlasting.

Surely in temples made with hands
God, the Most High, is not dwelling;
High above earth His temple stands,
All earthly temples excelling.
Yet He who dwells in heav'n above
Chooses to live with us in love,
Making our bodies His temple.

We are God's house of living stones,
Built for His own habitation.
He through baptismal grace us owns
Heirs of His wondrous salvation.
Were we but two His name to tell,
Yet He would deign with us to dwell
With all His grace and His favor.

Grant, then, O God, Your will be done,
That, when the church bells are ringing,
Many in saving faith may come
Where Christ His message is bringing;
"I know My own; My own know Me.
You, not the world, My face shall see.
My peace I leave with you. Amen."

Joy
Making Music

Chara

Greek for Joy
Divine happiness

Chapter Four

I PLAYED VIOLIN FROM FOURTH GRADE until high school, beginning with all the excitement of a new musician and ending with all the frustration of a distracted teen. Unlike band, which started a year later, orchestra began in the fourth grade, and wanting to be part of a select group of early musicians, I enthusiastically raised my hand to say I'd like to play. Soon I was sitting in the living room holding my prized rental. I was immediately entranced by the instrument with its smooth, polished wood, strings that resounded with notes I couldn't name, and the enchanting smell of rosin. I was in heaven.

As soon as orchestra started in school, my parents added private lessons and together with my tutor, we made beautiful music. My violin gave me a way to communicate: I could ground out scales or waltz into third position for a little Bach. By fifth grade I was ready to play in the spring talent show at school. I felt strong and confident in my ability and experienced sheer joy and delight in the music created.

In sixth grade Mom and Dad decided it was time to graduate from the rental to my very own instrument. My tutor went about making all the arrangements. Upon its arrival, we met and opened the shipping container together. I was filled with awe and wonder as the strings were tuned and she began to play. The beauty of this new violin was breathtaking. I was totally, deeply, and completely in love.

I never saw my tutor again. Unbeknownst to me, she was in the middle of a divorce and our time together that special afternoon was our last. Divorce was a difficult topic in 1965, so no word of explanation was ever given. I just knew that the person who had meant so much to me, who had shared with me the treasured gift of music, was gone. And she'd never even said goodbye.

A month later I started junior high and learned that orchestra would be held at the high school, a fifteen-minute bus ride away. We left at the end of fifth period and returned at the end of sixth. To accommodate this departure for the last period of the day, I was assigned to the slower track of the school's ability groupings. My two-hour morning block with struggling language arts students was brutal, but not half as agonizing as the trip to the high school later in the afternoon.

Our bus ride to orchestra practice was shared with eighth and ninth grade boys commuting to agriculture class, also at the high school. They were annoying and reeked of adolescent immaturity. Katie, another seventh grade violin student, and I tried desperately to ignore them, but to no avail. Mere minutes into our ride, I was longing for the simple, carefree days of grade school and questioning the need to make any kind of music anywhere, especially at the high school.

My doubts were reinforced as we entered the practice room to thirty faces, all showing a different look of displeasure. Not a single high school student expected this junior high/high school collaboration to be a benefit to anyone, least of all them. The unspoken challenge was to shut up, keep up, and perform—well, very well.

High school orchestra began with a difficult Vivaldi composition that the group had been working on for the last year and the piece that was expected to highlight our fall concert. I came home that first day frantic to begin private lessons anew, but Mom and Dad decided the extra expense wasn't necessary at that particular point in time. Without additional help, preparations for my first concert were incredibly hard and my entire first year of orchestra was horribly long.

Two years later I began private lessons with a college professor. Once a week I walked over to the music building on campus, just three blocks from home, but by now my interest in playing had started to wane. After a beginning that was memorable for all the wrong reasons, high school orchestra had become a test of endurance. I lasted until ninth grade and then decided that private lessons would be enough to sustain some kind of musical growth and development and perhaps recapture some degree of joy.

But by the time I quit orchestra, I had lost traction and my private lessons were as brutal as high school orchestra had been. Each week I would dash home from school right before my lesson, practice for forty-five minutes, and then try to pull something off with a smile and a complaint about the difficulty of an assigned etude. My professor knew differently. Before the third lesson, he was outlining his expectations of me as a student. With a halfhearted promise to practice, I renewed my vow to respect his time and my parents' financial support, sailing away for another week. Seven days later I was dashing home from school to practice for 45 minutes right before my lesson.

My professor tolerated my disinterest for a year. As I walked home from a lesson one dark winter afternoon, he called ahead to Mom and Dad and announced his firing of me as a violin student. Needless to say, they were not pleased; I, however, was dumbfounded. I knew he was frustrated with my inability to commit, I knew he was tired of my weekly excuses, but I was stunned that he had called my parents without saying a single word to me. In frustration and anger, I set my instrument aside and never touched it again.

Seven years later Mom and Dad sold my violin. Without a word, it was gone. Something that had meant so much to me, something that I had once treasured, was no longer part of my life. Mom and Dad had no way of knowing the mixed feelings I had for music. I never said a word as I wallowed in self-pity. What began as a joyous time ended in angst and pain. Even though I had no further interest in playing, I clung to a selfish need to decide my own musical fate, reacting with an ongoing "woe is me" attitude. I had struggled with loss, overwhelming expectations, and teenage distractions, and now I was reacting to another one of life's disappointments with the emotional maturity of an insolent child, stamping my feet because I hadn't gotten my own way.

With that, God gave me a thirty-year time-out. My Father in Heaven said, Enough! After one too many tantrums, He left me with the music of a car radio, old rock 'n' roll albums and a chance to sing in church, not pretty considering I have a five-note range.

Then one Sunday Elizabeth walked into church. A week later she was back with her oboe, playing throughout the service. I don't remember hearing a word of the sermon that morning. All I could think about was playing the violin as part of worship. Could I do it? Could I just walk in and play? God's answer came in the form of a well-worn violin rented a short time later. Instrument in hand, I joined Elizabeth and the pianist as a third member of the Sunday morning accompaniment. With her help, we found descants, worked together on duets, and got creative with our parts, nothing complicated, just special renditions of favorite songs and beautiful hymns.

Once again I became enchanted by the violin's feel and sound. But unlike fourth grade when a teacher asked me to play, this time God had extended the invitation. Together with Him, I found the joy that had eluded me for so long as I played for Him in His church, the highlight of my week and a moment of sheer joy.

God used my musical frustrations and disappointments to teach me about His joy. My own happiness had become entangled with life's shortcomings, leaving me sad and disheartened and feeling very sorry for myself. I looked back at the trying times through a filter of pain, seeing what I wanted to see (human failings), not what I needed to see (God's love and support). But then God met me in His house. Walking in with a young woman carrying an oboe, He re-introduced me to the music that I had once held so dear. On a beautiful sunny Sunday, He gave me back the feelings of promise and possibility I had first felt as a fourth grader. More importantly, He showed me the difference between my own personal happiness and divine joy, one fleeting and frequently overshadowed by life's heartaches, the other eternal and without compare.

When I was ready to graduate from a rental the second time, I went on a shopping adventure with my new teacher. Again, she made all the arrangements, this time meeting me at a grand old home filled with stringed instruments. I got to play and play until I found several that I liked. My teacher then played each one, allowing me to listen and to select the one that resonated most with both my head and my heart. Once again I was ten years old enjoying the breathtaking beauty of a new violin. I was totally, deeply, and completely in love.

I'm learning that divine joy comes from the seeds of hope given to me in God's unmerited love and complete forgiveness. As a member of His family, God replaced my fleeting moments of happiness with His joy, the fruit of His Holy Spirit. The memories of misunderstandings and misdeeds are reframed by a God who knew when to say enough, a God who was willing to wait patiently for my tantrums to subside, a God who was willing to give me another chance, another day, and another violin.

God showed me the difference between my happiness and His joy. In doing so, God put His joy inside a frame of love and forgiveness and then placed it back on the walls of my heart.

And now I pray:

Create in me a clean heart, O God, and renew a right spirit within me.
Cast me not away from your presence or take not your Holy Spirit from me.
Restore to me the joy of your salvation,
    and uphold me with a willing spirit.

—Psalm 51:10–12

With God, it can be so.

And by the way, while shopping for my second violin, I carefully examined the back of each instrument before playing. My first violin had been beautifully constructed with a back that was striking in its design and color but with a very small rough spot in the varnish. As I worked my way through violin after violin, I checked each for that rough spot. I couldn't help myself!

Joyful, Joyful We Adore You
Poem by Henry Van Dyke
Music by Samuel Sebastian Wesley

Joyful, joyful we adore Thee, God of glory, Lord of love,
Hearts unfold like flowers before Thee, hail Thee as the sun above.
Melt the clouds of sin and sadness, drive the dark of doubt away;
Giver of immortal gladness, fill us with the light of day.

All Thy works with joy surround Thee,
   earth and heav'n reflect Thy rays,
Stars and angels sing around Thee, center of unbroken praise;
Field and forest, vale and mountain, flow'ry meadow, flashing sea,
Changing birds and flowing fountain call us to rejoice in Thee.

Thou art giving and forgiving, ever blessing, ever blest,
Wellspring of the joy of living, ocean depth of happy rest.
Thou our Father, Christ our Brother, all who live in love are Thine;
Teach us how to love each other, lift us to the Joy Divine.

Mortals, join the mighty chorus, which the morning stars began,
Father love is reigning o'er us, brother love binds man to man.
Ever singing, march we onward, victors in the midst of strife;
Joyful music lifts us sunward, in the triumph song of life.

Kindness
Counseling

Chrestotes

Greek for Kindness and Goodness
A good or benevolent nature or disposition

Chapter Five

I MARRIED KURT AFTER DATING for almost nine years. Our on-again/off-again relationship became an engagement in the summer of 1980. As I began planning for the big event, Kurt graciously asked to be told the date, time, and place, deferring to my decisions throughout the preparations. I graciously took him at his word, proceeding to micromanage every aspect of every detail. I exhausted my mother and tested the patience and wallet of my father, but together we arranged for a wonderful day of love and celebration.

Kurt and I married in the Lutheran church where I was baptized and confirmed and where I had worked part-time as the weekend and summer secretary through high school and college. The sanctuary was just steps from the college where we'd met. Kurt's parents had known my parents while students at the same school, all graduating with teaching degrees. Twenty-three years later Kurt and I would graduate with the same plans to enter education. Our marriage brought together two families in the formation of an alumni conglomerate, which ultimately produced two sons. One would become a legacy student and the other would opt to go to any school but the family's ol' alma mater.

Our wedding was a happy occasion. I delighted in having our families together, reconnecting with high school friends and sharing the day with special people from every part of our lives. Being a "good Lutheran," I used the occasion to sing favorite hymns in a service that combined elements of Sunday morning worship and the marriage ceremony. It was a blessed hour that left many feeling they'd had enough church to last them for months. When one hymn was accidentally omitted, there was almost an audible sigh of relief.

Earlier, our pastor had asked to meet with Kurt and me for pre-marital counseling. I was not thrilled. I had a horrifying vision of failing some Lutheran compatibility test. After waiting for as long as I had, I didn't want to risk any incompatibility findings. Not worried about anything, Kurt just wanted to be told the date, time, and place for the actual event. Reluctantly, we met with the pastor for four Wednesday afternoons, praying the time would pass quickly and spare us from any awkward revelations.

Our counseling sessions were beyond the patience and understanding of two twenty-somethings. We met in Pastor's office where he sat at his desk while we sat on a low couch that left us just beneath his line of sight. With the afternoon sun shining through the windows behind him, we found ourselves blinded by a shockingly bright vision that blurred his head and left his face indistinguishable. When he spoke, I thought of Moses listening to God's voice coming from the burning bush on Mt. Sinai. This image was quickly replaced with a vision of God's people in the desert, people who had been blessed with manna from heaven and who had responded with one complaint after another. Like the Israelites in that story, I was feeling very unappreciative. Even though I had been blessed by God beyond measure, I was feeling put upon that I had to spend a whole hour for four consecutive weeks learning how to make the most of His wonderful gift of marriage. As I sat next to the man who had asked me to be his wife, the very man who was willing to put up with me and all my idiosyncrasies, all I could think about were the minutes remaining in the session and the many things I felt I needed to be doing at that exact moment.

Premarital counseling had to be an interesting part of Pastor's job description. Was the man responsible for leading a large suburban church of feisty European descent really expected to advise and counsel those too clueless to know what they didn't know? Like so many, we actually sat before him thinking we knew it all, but having absolutely no idea what lay ahead. Where would he begin? How would he share the lessons of a lifetime with two people who thought they were ready for anything, one just wondering if the florist had called back and the other just wanting to know the date, time, and place?

Pastor's response to the counseling dilemma was to make his discussions very general and conceptual, but for us, this created a new problem: Presented with these broad, sweeping topics, we had difficulty understanding his point each week. The gist of his messages sailed right over our heads. When he finally got to sex, it took us most of the hour before we understood what he was trying to say and by then we had to avoid eye contact with each other, fearing our deterioration into very un-Lutheran-like laughter.

Despite the perceived failings of our premarital instruction, Kurt and I left with simple, yet profound advice: "Try every day to do something unexpected, something special, something unspoken and unselfish for the other person." Thanks to the pastor, not a day goes by that I haven't been the benefactor of an act of kindness as I enjoy life with a man who continues to shower me with his grace. Some days it's a kind word; other days it's a clean car with a full tank of gas. Some days it's the patience to listen as I rant about the insignificant; other days it's a calm, sincere reassurance of my skills and abilities. Every day it's something—just for me.

Kurt's acts of kindness extend far beyond his wife. He genuinely tries to make this world a kinder, gentler place. It's so much a part of who he is that I'm not sure he's even aware of it. He goes the extra mile. He believes in the good in everyone. When he says, "It's a great day in Monroe," he truly means it, and if he hasn't said it out loud, he's thinking it.

After surviving the chapter on love, I assured Kurt the rest of the book would be my own stories, that he wouldn't have to cringe at the thought of becoming roadkill on Deanna's "memory lane." But Kurt's kindness is a big part of my story. Through him and his unselfish participation in life, I have learned to be a better person. He doesn't complete me. He's not my better half. He's my inspiration. As his wife, I want to be the best I can be. I want to become a loving, joyous, peaceful, patient, kind, good, faithful, gentle, self-controlled delight in God's eyes, praying that with His fruit, I can become a loving, joyous, peaceful, patient, kind, good, faithful, gentle, self-controlled delight in Kurt's life. It's the least I can do and the most I can hope and pray for.

Through Kurt I learned to forgive. Growing up, I could pout for weeks on end from the smallest slight. Kurt taught me to forgive and forget. Kurt's kindness is not about "being nice;" it's about loving others enough to forgive their failings and shortcomings. He wipes the slate clean; he gives an unconditional pardon. Nothing is ever dredged up. No words will ever belie an earlier frustration or disappointment. Mistakes are erased and do-overs allowed.

Seeing the fruit of God's Spirit in Kurt, I can begin to understand and appreciate the enormity of God's kindness and His own love for me. God truly forgives and forgets—everything, every day, in every way. He has wiped my own record clean and He continues to absolve me of my sins "in thought, word, and deed," those wrongdoings, shortcomings, imperfections, and transgressions that plagued me in the pew. I can look back and know that each and every sin, large or small, is forever erased. One pastor said it was like having God as my judge and Jesus as my defense counsel. Knowing I was up on capital offenses, God arranged for my defense, making sure I got the best representation, His Son. I was brought before God damned by The Law, charged with failing to keep His Word through my deeds. Jesus, my Lord and my Savior, not only spoke on my behalf, He and God agreed on a plea deal where He assumed my guilt and accepted my punishment. I got life without parole, life now and for eternity.

I was the prodigal daughter, the lost soul who wanted to see the world, who thought she knew it all, who wanted earthly delights now, in lieu of heavenly rewards later. Waiting patiently, protecting my place in His family, God, my Father, welcomed my return with open arms. God knew I would screw up, but I am not a screw-up. I am His. God created a special place for me in His family. God surrounded me with all of the fruits of His Holy Spirit, making each one a part of my own spirit. Seeing me in the middle of a three-week pout, He planned a divine intervention. Seeing me wander off course, He took me down roads I would not have chosen, all leading back to Him. He placed people in my life that I never expected to meet, all helping me to see Him more clearly.

Reframing the past has created a beautiful new understanding of my Father, His Son, and Holy Spirit. With the glass polished, I can see His love and kindness, the forgiveness, mercy, and grace that have been there all along. And now with His help, I am able to share that kindness with family and friends and all His people.

At the end of our wedding ceremony, we asked the congregation to share in a prayer on our behalf. Today it remains my prayer:

O God, my Creator, I rejoice that You are with us, fulfilling Your promise in every age. Look with grace upon Kurt and me as we continue to love You and each other. Give to us the peace, joy, and love that You have for all those whom You bring together in Your kingdom. Help us to affirm our love, strengthening the oneness we have with each other. As You love us, may we love one another—freely, generously. Bless our life together that it may fulfill Your purpose. In Christ's name, Amen.

After our wedding rehearsal, accompanied by the wedding party, we headed out to Jim's 21 21 for a pitcher of beer and some pool and darts. Nine years later we were back at the place where it all began, evidence that God either has a terrific sense of humor or an indulgent side of Him that rarely gets acknowledged.

Praise to the Lord, the Almighty

Words by Joachim Neander, translated by Catherine Winkworth
Music from the Ander Theil Des Erneuerten Gesang-Buchs

Praise to the Lord, the Almighty, the King of creation!
O my soul, praise Him, for He is your health and salvation!
Let all who hear
Now to His temple draw near,
Joining in glad adoration!

Praise to the Lord, who o'er all things is wondrously reigning
And, as on wings of an eagle, uplifting, sustaining.
Have you not seen
All that is needful has been
Sent by His gracious ordaining?

Praise to the Lord, who has fearfully, wondrously, made you,
Health has bestowed and, when heedlessly falling, has stayed you.
What need or grief
Ever has failed of relief?
Wings of his mercy did shade you.

Praise to the Lord, who will prosper your work and defend you;
Surely His goodness and mercy shall daily attend you.
Ponder anew
What the Almighty can do
As with His love he befriends you.

Praise to the Lord! O let all that is in me adore Him!
All that has life and breath, come now with praises before Him!
Let the Amen
Sound from His people again;
Gladly forever adore Him!

Goodness
Having Children

Chrestotes

Greek for kindness and Goodness
The best part of anything

Chapter Six

I GAVE BIRTH TO OUR FIRST SON, Kyle on my thirtieth birthday. Not only did he and I share the day, but we also shared the same time of arrival at minutes before 3:00 AM. His birth came two weeks after my due date on the day I had actually selected since it sounded fun. I never expected to be waiting two very long weeks for a very overdue baby. By the time Kyle was born, I was initially more relieved than excited to be forever sharing a celebratory event. Two and a half years later my second son Kevin made his own entrance into the world. Kevin was born just before Christmas, again two weeks late. After arriving on their own schedules, I knew my impact on their future comings and goings would be marginal at best.

I was awed that God had selected me to be the mother of two delightful little boys. God had entrusted me to nurture them, to guide and protect them, to raise them as His own. He knew my cooking skills would favor nutritionally questionable boxes of macaroni and cheese. He knew my patience would fail miserably on long, hot afternoons. He knew my children would outgrow naps before I did. And yet He chose me to love and mother them.

I must have done something good.

The officer who pulled me over didn't think so. With lights flashing and siren shrieking, he stopped me on my way home from work one afternoon when the boys were small. After I parked on the side of the interstate, he walked up to my window, took one look at two toddlers in car seats, and launched into a diatribe on responsible parenting. It was bad enough that I was speeding on the freeway using an expired license, but with small children buckled in beside me, he had more than enough fuel for a dissertation on my irresponsibility as a mother. I cried uncontrollably. As two startled little faces looked on, I nodded my responses to the police officer's questions, unable to speak. He had no idea how far I'd come!

Years earlier on a Friday morning during my second year of teaching, I was caught speeding the last few blocks before school in a valiant attempt to make it to class on time. Again with lights flashing, the officer signaled for me to pull over. With no place to stop, I entered the school parking lot. There in front of everyone, I grimaced as I got out of the car and began a difficult encounter with one of the city's finest. The front of the school building was a wall of glass from one end to the other, so those in the administrative offices, teachers' lounge, and several classrooms got to watch me struggle through a rapidly deteriorating situation. I was ticketed for going 50-plus in a 25 mph zone, an automatic reckless driving charge. I was also racing through a school zone, so Reckless Driving with a capital R and a capital D. As Alexander would have said, "It was a terrible, horrible, no good, very bad day!"

The reckless driving charge was expensive. As a beginning schoolteacher, the amount of the fine was well beyond my ability to pay. Not sure what to do, I called the courthouse and asked for help: "Do you have an easy payment plan?" The clerk asked if I was at fault and remembering all forty sets of eyes that fateful morning, I replied that I was. Six weeks later I went to court and pleaded guilty in a "trial by declaration," promising a judge that I would keep my foot off the gas for a six-month probationary period. I left after paying court costs and a nominal fee. I was also breathing a grateful sigh of relief.

Compared to that reckless driving charge, my stop on the interstate was minor. The officer just didn't understand, but then after a slow drive home, I came to realize that he understood all too well. God had given me two precious sons and I was treating His gift carelessly—and yes, irresponsibly. Through an angry police officer, God had spoken to me. I was mortified and humbled and instantly resolved to do better.

Not every day was as dramatic, but parenting was challenging nonetheless. By the time I gained a reasonable amount of experience and a degree of expertise in any particular aspect of childrearing, the boys entered a new phase, leaving me struggling anew. I read books, I participated in Mommy and Me groups, I listened to an angry police officer. I worked hard to make sure that I was the best mom possible, imparting every ounce of wisdom I had or thought I had. But looking back, I see now that the lessons my sons shared with me were infinitely more valuable. Parenting was truly God's gift of goodness to me, providing lessons I'll treasure and remember forever.

Lessons in Goodness

Don't huddle up in baseball

While Kurt was coaching Kyle's sixth grade baseball team, I "helped" as his bench coach. I gave the boys batting tips and delightful words of encouragement before they headed out to home plate. Facing our opponent's best pitcher during the last game of the season, I called for a huddle before the next at-bat, sharing with them the news that they had been facing the other team's "Randy Johnson." Thinking they were encouraged and inspired, I watched our players march out to the plate one by one and stand absolutely motionless, never blinking, never swinging, each one caught looking. They retired our side after just three batters. I learned that teams huddle up in football, not baseball.

There is a time for everything, and a season for every activity under heaven.

–Ecclesiastes 3:1

All in good time, the saying goes. More accurately it's all in God's time, God's time and place. I joke that I am always available should God need help with His timing, should He want to huddle up before His next at bat. I've even offered "helpful" suggestions as I've struggled with His will for me and my life. God simply shakes His head and makes a note to "bless" me with another lesson in trust and patience. Looking back, there is no denying that God's timing was infinitely better than my own at every point in life, and the blessings that flowed were immeasurably greater than anything I could have hoped for or planned for in one of life's huddles.

Don't be weird

After completing my term as secretary for our church leadership group, I became the coordinator for our middle school youth program, a worrisome situation for our resident seventh grader. When asked how I was doing after the first two meetings, Kyle replied, "You're doing OK, Mom. Just don't be weird." Later in high school, Kyle had his father for U.S. History. A couple weeks into the semester, I asked Kyle how it was going. He replied, "You know, Mom, Dad does a pretty good job." Kurt and I found it very reassuring that after teaching for more than twenty-five years, he'd just survived one of his toughest evaluations.

It was he who gave some to be apostles, some to be prophets, some to be evangelists, and some to be pastors and teachers.

—Ephesians 4:11

God has given me many opportunities to serve Him and His people, at times a particularly challenging situation as I sorted through life's to-dos and God's call. And if I'm honest, I have to admit that I have worked hard at times to find the easiest activity, by any particular day's definition, in order to avoid the greater challenge: bringing others to Christ. I have feared that walking with God meant walking down the street knocking on doors with a Bible in one hand and a pamphlet in the other, but God had other plans for me. He gave me a life, not a route. With skills and abilities that are truly gifts from above, God enabled me to be a witness to His love and mercy in all that I do, whether coaching or leading, whether being Kurt's wife or Kyle and Kevin's mom, whether in a huddle or with a youth group. Called into His service, I was set apart. I was different. Contrary to the opinion of two teenagers, I wasn't weird, a little annoying perhaps, but not weird. I was God's child. Life only got weird when distractions separated me from God and His family, when I distanced myself from His will, when I chose to follow my own path, not His.

Don't assume you know everything

In sixth grade Kyle began an independent study in math. One week he completed Chapter 5 on Wednesday, Chapter 7 on Thursday, and Chapter 8 on Friday. Worried about Chapter 6, I expressed concern, remembering that even in the good ol' days of "new math," 6 came between 5 and 7. Kyle responded in his nicest "I'm going to humor you" voice, "I skipped it, Mom."

And this is my prayer: that your love may abound more and more in knowledge and depth of insight, so that you may be able to discern what is best and may be pure and blameless until the day of Christ, filled with the fruit of righteousness that comes through Jesus Christ—to the glory and praise of God.

—Philippians 1:9–11

As a mother, I had days that were absolutely memorable and others that were regrettably trying. Before children, I considered myself smart, talented, resourceful, a good rugged individualist. After children, I was reminded that every day was a new opportunity to make (or not make) a wonderful impact on the life of my sons, so I was going to need an extra measure of smarts, talents, and resources. I could no longer be that rugged individualist. I needed help. I had to have a relationship with God. I needed more than books on parenting; I needed His Word on living. I needed more than *Sesame Street* to help with early childhood growth and development; I needed to grow as a child of God myself, so I could help two little boys grow as children of God. Knowing that, God surrounded me with the most remarkable family and church family who nurtured and sustained me.

Don't miss the news

In fourth grade when Kevin completed his *Weekly Reader* in an unusually short period of time, I nicely asked to see his work, knowing he couldn't have mastered articles on the Gulf War syndrome and the rescue of fishermen in the Pacific so quickly. When I expressed shock and amazement at the accuracy of his answers, he quickly reminded me that both stories had been on TV: "You just have to watch the news, Mom!"

He who has ears, let him hear.
—Matthew 11:15, 13:9, 43

God has spoken to me in so many different ways. An insightful song begins, "Listen! Listen, God is calling." Often I've found it easy to get so focused on the minutia before me that I've missed the bigger picture. It's been said that God is in the details, but He's also in the people, places, and things surrounding me every day. I can multitask with the best of them, but in the middle of doing ten things, I miss the one big thing: God's will for me that moment, that day. I am reminded that I need to listen and pay attention, never knowing where God will want and need to connect with me. It might be in the voice of a friend or the words of a daily devotional. I've asked God for sticky notes on the refrigerator, wanting to be sure I got every message, but after giving me His Word, I think it's time to put up my own sticky notes.

Don't give the keys to an underage boy

After his band concert, I handed Kyle the keys to the car, needing a few minutes to finish cleaning up before meeting him. Too many minutes later I strolled out toward the school parking lot, thinking I heard a car running, a car that sounded a lot like the our Caprice. To my horror, it was the Caprice with my fifth grader behind the wheel! "But, Mom, I just needed to listen to the radio."

God, who has called you into fellowship with his Son Jesus Christ our Lord is faithful.
—1 Corinthians 1:9

Even on my best days as a mother, I needed another set of hands, another pair of eyes, a longer nap. Through it all God was with me and my family. He comforted and protected; He supported and encouraged. He was my second set of hands. And when I took too long to get to the parking lot, He sat in the passenger seat as my ten-year-old listened to the radio, keeping his hands on the dials and off the gearshift.

Don't overlook the wisdom that surrounds you

Kevin is wise beyond his years. In my former life before marriage and children, I was politically active and tried to keep up with the issues of the day, especially as they related to education. As a young mother, I remember sitting on the curb at the high school one dark afternoon waiting for Kurt to finish football practice. I was crying, because I had my Voters' Guide in hand and didn't know who and what to vote for: "I used to know this stuff!" Kurt sat with me and patiently talked through the candidates and the issues, leaving me acutely aware that life had forever changed with the birth of two children. Today the younger of my two sons is my go-to guy for political advice and counsel. What I have to work so hard to grasp and understand, he absorbs and digests with ease. And more importantly, like his father, he's willing to patiently talk it through with me.

My son, if you accept my words and store up my commands within you, turning your ear to wisdom and applying your heart to understanding, and if you call out for insight and cry aloud for understanding, and if you look for it as for silver and search for it as for hidden treasure, then you will understand the fear of the Lord and find the knowledge of God.

—Proverbs 2:1–5

Wisdom is more than being smart. As I become more knowledgeable in the ways of God, I am able to apply His teachings to life with greater ease and spiritually satisfying results. But to do that, I need to study His Word, and I've avoided opening my Bible more times than I care to admit. Rather than look at the Old and New Testaments as a glorious resource, I let the page count become a stumbling block. Rather than trust that God will lead me in my study, I go knit. Forever faithful, God refuses to let me slip away, giving me a new day, surrounding me with new ways in which to know and love Him. Some days He helps me write and some days He just sits beside me as I knit—with a wonderful Bible study at my side.

God's goodness is truly the best part of anything, and the goodness He has shared with me and my family is more far ranging and more blessed than I could have dreamed possible. Kyle and Kevin truly represent the very best of my relationship with Kurt. Through God's love and forgiveness, I was able to be a great mom, not a perfect mom, but a great mom just for them.

And to the sons of the mother with questionable cooking skills, God gave divine culinary abilities. And for that I thank God. I must have done something good!

And I pray this in order that I may live a life worthy of You, Lord, and may please You in every way: bearing fruit in every good work, growing in the knowledge of You, being strengthened with all power according to Your glorious might so that I may have great endurance and patience, and joyfully give thanks to You, my Father, who has qualified me to share in the inheritance of the saints in the kingdom of light.

—based on Colossians 1:10–12

With God it can be so.

Remembering our premarital counseling, I thought about sending the pastor a quick note: "Just tell prospective couples that everything they'll need to know about life and each other, they'll learn with God's help as parents." I just thought it might free up his Wednesday afternoons.

Now Thank We All Our God
Words by Martin Rinckart, translated by Catherine Winkworth
Music by Johann Cruger

Now thank we all our God With hearts and hands and voices,
Who wondrous things has done, In whom His world rejoices;
Who from our mothers' arms Has blest us on our way
With countless gifts of love And still is ours today.

Oh, my this bounteous God Through all our life be near us,
With ever joyful hearts And blessed peace to cheer us
And keep us in His grace And guide us when perplexed
And free us from all ills In this world and the next!

All praise and thanks to God The Father how be given,
The Son, and Him who reigns With them in highest heaven,
The one eternal God, Whom earth and heav'n adore;
For this it was, is now, And will be evermore.

Patience
Enduring Pain

Makrothumia or Hupomone

Greek for Patience
The ability to endure
under difficult circumstances

Chapter Seven

I TESTED THE PATIENCE of my entire family. In high school, if I was asked to be home at midnight, I would drive around the block eight times and make sure I walked in the back door at 12:15 AM. If I was asked to come straight home, I added three stops to my drive. For fifty years I charged through life in my own way at my own speed in my own time, and then hip and knee issues took their toll. As my knees degenerated into bone-on-bone pain, my hip did its best to compensate. Again the result was bone-on-bone agony. I had trouble walking. My stamina disappeared overnight. I found myself out of breath with a couple stairs or a few extra steps. Sunday afternoons I would cry in frustration and pain after struggling through a Sunday morning worship service with a few stand-ups and sit-downs. And to make myself feel better, I ate my way through an additional fifty pounds, trying with bite after bite to nurture and comfort myself. I knew I couldn't swallow away the pain, but still I ate, grabbing anything to feel better. Carbs and chocolate became my drugs of choice. The resulting poundage only added to my problems, finding me now officially "obese" and my joints struggling anew.

I railed at God. Not only was I trying my best to be a good wife and mother, but I was trying hard to be a good leader in my neighborhood church, His church. I served as its treasurer, I played violin on Sundays, I led a women's group and facilitated a book club. I promoted Christian fellowship with special parties. Had God forgotten all that I'd done?

In my church life I had thoroughly enjoyed finding ways in which to bring God's people together. At the suggestion of a young woman, we started our women's Caring in Sharing group. Together with many wonderful ladies, we studied God's Word and then knitted and crocheted special gifts for the sick and shut-in. Every Monday I was blessed with their friendship and wisdom. They entrusted me with their prayers. We laughed together and then finished the evening with some delectable bite of chocolate.

God had also inspired me to start the Light Reading book club. Each month we enjoyed a fiction or nonfiction book chosen to help us grow in the light of Christ. Attendance at our meetings varied. In addition to a good discussion, the promise of a latte at the local coffee shop always boosted participation. I delighted in seeing the stack of our latest selection disappear month after month with books reappearing among church members and others, even showing up in the community. I smiled one afternoon while working out, seeing one of our books with someone on an exercise bike at the gym. I got emotional when one of our older members said he'd never read a book cover to cover until he saw the book on Martin Luther's wife. His own daughter was a Lutheran pastor's wife and he appreciated the story and the chance to connect with her through the life of Kitty Luther.

Highlighting my volunteer endeavors were Friendship Sundays. Our pastor suggested having a birthday party for our oldest members. I took the idea a step further and made it a special celebration of each life, something we did for more and more of our seniors over the next few years. We incorporated favorite Bible verses and hymns in the worship service and then gathered for a reception in their honor. I had the pleasure and good fortune to visit with each one of them, collecting stories for a special handout that day. After one particular celebration, a high school student stopped me in the church kitchen. He was so excited: "Deanna, did you know that Lester fought in the war? He was part of World War II in the Pacific!" I responded that I had written the story, hearing the details firsthand. He was speechless.

Then one November evening I told my Caring in Sharing friends that I could no longer continue. By the end of the day I had no energy. I told them I was overwhelmed by pain. What I didn't tell them was that I was so inwardly focused, I could no longer reach out. Again I railed at God. How could He take me away from the place where I was needed most—His church? How could He separate me from the place I most wanted to be? I had no time or patience for failing body parts.

Pain cost me the ability to walk with any degree of ease. I was crushed. Since college I had found walking to be a wonderful way to get outside and enjoy the fresh air. For someone who didn't like to sweat, it was the perfect answer to cardiovascular activity. With care and attention, I could elevate my heart rate without sacrificing a single bead of perspiration. It was perfect!

When the boys were small we rarely missed our daily walk together—around the block, around town, in the rain, in the sun. After graduating from naps, this time together became a gift, a short midday break for Mom. Together we talked and enjoyed the sights. Some afternoons we ran a couple errands; occasionally we stopped and said hello to Kurt after football practice. The day we got a new Radio Flyer, I was so excited that I grabbed a two-year old Kevin and immediately set out for a short walk/ride around the block. All went well until the final corner when I realized he'd fallen out of the wagon twenty yards earlier. I found him upside down in a heap at the side of the road, too stunned to cry. As I brushed off the gravel and reassured Kevin that all was fine, I took a quick look around to see how many neighbors were making note of the sorry situation. Fortunately most of our time on the streets was less newsworthy and required fewer Band-Aids.

After years of walking with the boys, walking alone, and walking with Kurt, I now found myself walking with great discomfort and lacking the endurance for even basic activities. I continued to whine, questioning God's love and support. I understood that the hip joint was beyond rehabilitation. What started as a knee issue was now a hip joint needing to be replaced. What I didn't understand was the lack of divine intervention. Why would God take me from the work I loved— work in His church—and sit me on the couch in misery? Why would He stop all the good I relished doing on His behalf?

When I finally got my new hip, I waited and waited—some days patiently, but many days impatiently—for the pain to stop and my strength to return. I walked and ran laps in the pool, I walked around the cul-de-sac, I tried to do a little weight training. When the discomfort increased, I opted for a Monday-Wednesday-Friday schedule of exercise, giving my body time to rest between activities. After eight months, my patience was gone. Hearing once again, "Deanna, you're recovering from major surgery," left me disheartened and discouraged. I just knew my recovery had to be outside the norm, but the experts continued to tell me otherwise.

Fourteen months after my surgery, the replacement joint was recalled after patients reported problems with pain, swelling, and difficulty walking. I was relieved and devastated. I quickly addressed invitations to a pity party, including everyone I knew and loved. I made it a point to arrive early and stay late. I dressed in misery and sadness. I was a one-person show of self-indulgence and preoccupation with self.

To the outside observer, the analogy is exaggerated. Few had any idea that I was so disheartened. The struggles were within me—and with God. I just didn't understand the need to continue limping through life. I really felt I had a good understanding of my skills and abilities, appreciating the ways in which I could contribute to God's work. As I pulled back from activities, I saw the bigger picture. I saw beyond my own particular experience to a greater good. Being a rather vocal and at times formidable force, stepping aside allowed others to step forward. I understood and appreciated the changes. Was the recall of a bad hip joint really necessary?

In the time it took to read the recall notification, I lost every last ounce of hope and determination. I was swearing by the time I got to the second paragraph. Later that afternoon, a re-reading brought me to tears. By now the feelings of relief were waning ("So there's a reason...") and waves of fear and anger were overwhelming me ("I can't go through surgery again!").

And then our new pastor arrived.

And then our new pastor started his Weekly Email Encouragement.

And then our new pastor sent an electronic devotional titled, "Surviving the Lions!"

I don't think that there is one person (who) I have ever met who has been exempted from hard times in life. There is a misbelief in much of Christianity that once you experience the Kingdom of God in your life and Jesus becomes intensely real to you that you are "protected" from tough times....People interpret the "abundant life" that Jesus promises as if Jesus was around to insulate us from reality. It just doesn't happen, does it? For those who trust in Jesus, we echo what David wrote when he penned those famous words in the 23rd Psalm:

When I walk through the valley of the shadow of death,
I shall fear no evil for You are with me, God.
—Psalm 23

Note he doesn't write "if" I walk through the valley. He exclaims "when."
Hard times are inevitable and to be anticipated. It is part of what it means to
live in a broken world.

And then the light went on.

Maybe the question wasn't "Why me?" Perhaps the question was "Why not me?" I was born with knees and a hip that would ultimately have a shorter life span than other body parts. My genetics, my choice of activities, and my age resulted in a major skeletal collision at three joints. Strewn amongst the wreckage was a painful left knee, a damaged right knee, and a badly deteriorated hip. Fortunately for me, God answered the 911 call, arriving first on the scene. He pulled me from the wreckage and got me into the care of a capable surgeon, dynamic physical therapist, and compassionate primary care physician.

And He never left my side. As my body struggled to heal, God added to the team of people caring for me. As I sunk into the darkness of depression and self-pity, He spoke through a new pastor, a shepherd who shared the words of another shepherd, providing the encouragement I desperately needed.

Today I have a genuine empathy, understanding, and patience for people in pain. So often I looked past a limp, ignored the cane. I lived with a twenty-year-old's belief that the body was ageless, and then I began to limp and use a cane. An attitude of superiority separated me from the sufferings of others, and then I lost my identity to chronic discomfort and found myself unable to do and to be. I scorned the overweight, and then I gained fifty-six pounds. God replaced my humiliation, misunderstandings, and mistaken judgments with a grateful heart and a spirit of kindness, gentleness—and even a little patience.

And so I pray:

May today there be peace within.
May I trust that I am exactly where I am meant to be.
May I not forget the infinite possibilities that are born of faith.
May I use those gifts that I have received,
    and pass on the love that has been given to me.
May I be content knowing that I am a child of God.
May this knowledge settle into my bones,
    and allow my soul the freedom to sing, dance, praise and love.
It is there for each and every one of us.

                                        –based on the Prayer St. Theresa of Avila

With God it can be so.

We're not promised a rose garden, but "God gave His children memory that in life's garden there might be June roses in December." Knowing that God has been with me every minute—in the stubbornness of my youth and in the pain and frustration of an aging adult, I remember in gratitude all that He has done for me and all that He continues to do. The roses He has shared still smell as sweet. It's a beautiful picture of love and care.

My Hope Is Built on Nothing Less
Words by John Bacchus Dykes
Music by Edward Mote

My hope is built on nothing less
Than Jesus' Blood and righteousness;
No merit of my own I claim,
But wholly lean on Jesus' Name.
On Christ, the solid rock, I stand;
All other ground is sinking sand.

When darkness veils His lovely face
I rest on His unchanging grace;
In every high and stormy gale
My anchor holds within the veil.
On Christ, the solid rock, I stand;
All other ground is sinking sand.

His oath, His covenant, His Blood,
Support me in the whelming flood;
When all around my soul gives way,
He then is all my hope and stay.
On Christ, the solid rock, I stand;
All other ground is sinking sand.

When He shall come with trumpet sound,
O may I then in Him be found,
Dressed in His righteousness alone,
Faultless to stand before the throne!
On Christ, the solid rock, I stand;
All other ground is sinking sand.

Gentleness
Bingeing

Praotes

Greek for Gentleness
Strength under control

Chapter Eight

I BEGAN WRITING OUT OF DESPAIR. I think I was hoping that by putting words on paper, I might discover the truth about what ailed me. After fighting with my body for decades, I was fretting over body fat that seemed to expand exponentially by the second. My memories of afternoon wagon rides with the boys were being pushed aside by the vision of Oprah crossing the stage with her wagonload of pounds lost, an episode in TV history that was beginning to haunt me as I jumped on the scale for the ninth time since breakfast. I wanted desperately to fill my own wagon with fifty-six pounds of excess weight, fifty-six ridiculous pounds. I was frantic to save any remnants of an ego hurt by shame and frustration. I remembered my own mother's struggle with weight and finally had to admit that I was heavier than she had ever been. I narrowed my circle of friends and activities, not wanting to face my skinny past, not wanting to risk a "What happened to her?" encounter. I tried to tell myself that my struggle with weight began with the pain of deteriorating joints, but it really began long ago in high school as a dreadful cycle of bingeing and purging. My Type A perfectionism just didn't mesh with the messiness of teenage angst and a young woman's struggle for identity.

My high school experience actually began beautifully—in a brand-new, ultramodern facility of round buildings just down the hill from where I lived. It was 1969. As Neil Armstrong set foot on the moon, we prepared to set foot on a new campus. In keeping with the theme we walked into new educational models that included a school calendar of semesters separated by an interim month, and a class schedule with a day for large group instruction followed by four days of classroom work. We were introduced to a novel concept called "independent study." We ate lunch from vending machines. But despite the advancements, the dress code was still dresses, some short, some impossibly short, the bane of school administrators who were armed with rulers ready to measure offending hemlines in a determined effort to maintain a sense of decency and decorum.

As a sophomore, my class schedule included English, Social Studies, Geometry, Typing, German, and P.E., a generic course load for a period in time that was loud and disconcerting to some and intense and challenging to others. Two weeks after a music festival in Woodstock, New York, I sauntered into first period English. As opposition to the Vietnam War grew more hostile and race riots continued to erupt, I grabbed the third seat in the second row and settled in for *Twelve Angry Men.* I sat directly behind Ben, a nice enough guy who added a little levity to an otherwise trying first fifty minutes of the day. Even though I would graduate from college with a major in English, my zeal for in-depth literary analyses was never a strength nor a passion. Ben kept things light. As soon as we entered class each day, the banter began. We harangued each other about the homework, teased each other about the inability to come through with yesterday's answer to a discussion question, and threatened to reveal each other's dread of everything English.

Late in the first semester a special informal dance was to be held where the girls got to invite the boys. As I considered possible dates, Ben seemed like the logical choice, not because I was particularly interested in him, but because he made me laugh. I figured we could spend the evening delighting in our escape from book reviews and the diagramming of sentences. Deciding to ask Ben was the easy part. The harder/hardest part was actually asking him. I stressed for weeks. I rehearsed my script in front of the bathroom mirror; I worked on my delivery as I walked to school each day. As time got short, I finally had to act. Following Ben out of class one morning, I stopped at his locker and blurted out my invitation. With all my self-confidence forgotten back in the classroom in that third seat of the second row, my voice came out in a shrill rasp eight octaves above normal with my breathing reduced to quick, painful gasps. Watching me struggle, listening intently, Bill finally responded, proudly announcing that he had a girlfriend at another school and would be going to her dance.

A *girlfriend!* How could we have spent weeks—no, months—together and the mention of a girlfriend never came up, not once? How could we have been so focused on stupid classroom stuff that we never got around to likes and dislikes, like girlfriends? And now—how many people had just seen this regrettable display of rejection in the middle of the hallway? I was devastated! If only I'd run my idea past a friend or two. Surely someone would have mentioned a girlfriend. I didn't even like Ben! I just wanted to go to the dance. He wasn't even that cool! But he was obviously cooler than I was, since he had a dance to go to and I didn't. My weeks of anxiety were for naught, and now my ability to cope, my ability to smile and say "No problem! See you in class tomorrow!" evaporated in a millisecond.

At that point in my short life, experience with love and romance was abbreviated and hyphenated, as in very short and only semi-memorable. I still nurtured a crush on a neighborhood classmate, an elementary school fantasy that remained out of reach and a "not in this lifetime" proposition. Back in sixth grade I'd decided on Paul McCartney as my favorite Beatle and Dan as my too-cute-for-words crush. As far as I was concerned, he really was too cute for words. I hardly remember talking to him, only daydreaming about him. Years later I would walk into him, literally, at our ten-year high school reunion. In the middle of a rented ballroom, I was back in sixth grade, giggling at the sight of him, too embarrassed to speak. A few years later we met again at a business meeting. This time I was actually able to put together a brief, yet coherent introduction, "Hi, I'm Deanna Nowadnick. My maiden name was Thorp." His reply? "Do I know you? Did we go to school together?" My crush from elementary school didn't even remember me.

Before asking Ben to the dance, the only other occasion worth mentioning came at the end of ninth grade. Wanting to go to our graduation dance more than anyone wanted to ask me, I allowed friends to set me up on a date. The results were disastrous. Forgetting that I was dateless because the good options had already made their selections, I had neglected to consider the remaining possibilities. My surprise came at the festivities when I walked into the actual setup. There in front of me was a delighted Grant. There I stood absolutely mortified. *Not Grant! He was weird. He was really, really weird. What had I been thinking? Why had I consented to this ridiculous proposition?*

By the time I asked Ben to the dance, I was ready to take matters into my own hands, moving beyond a preteen's crush and the "blind" encounter, but Ben's turndown meant that even my own efforts had failed me. I went home and ate ten saltines dripping in raspberry jam, six large marshmallows, four stale graham crackers, and a bowl of ice cream with chocolate sauce and nuts—and promptly threw up. My fifteen-year-old response to a minor setback became a full-blown bulimic episode. The binge soothed my hurting ego; the purge brought forth years of stuffed emotions. What I failed to appreciate at that moment and in the afternoons to come was how my cycle of bingeing and purging would further exacerbate the problem for years to come, never providing any real comfort, any real control. The child who felt she had no voice had finally spoken and the results were disheartening. The young girl who had been unable to express her emotions had grown into a teen with absolutely no ability to cope with her feelings—good, bad, or indifferent. And any chance at keeping life in perspective was now overruled by hormones.

My extreme efforts remained a deep, dark secret. Even though I knew my behavior was out of my control, I couldn't stop. I was reeling in self-loathing. In 1972 if someone had said that I had an eating disorder, I would have replied, "A *what?*" The word wasn't even part of my vernacular. Afraid and alone, I believed my actions, my inability to cope had to be kept from everyone. No one could know. I became the master of disguise, smiling on the outside, spinning out of control on the inside. I was ashamed and fearful. I was mortified at the thought of being discovered, yet not even the shame of my actions could keep me from my afternoon "escapes."

For twenty years my days were characterized by an unwavering determination, troublesome strength, and misdirected resolve. By my early thirties I finally admitted to the "disorder" of my eating. With two little boys before me, I accepted God's wake-up call and opened my eyes to my dysfunctional behavior. Still ashamed and fearful, I faced a new clear and present danger: What if I should transfer—consciously or unconsciously—the wrong message about food and life to my two sons? In tears I called Kurt and said I needed to get help. I began group counseling, with individual counseling added years later. Each session brought renewed efforts to connect with my emotions. Then I awakened to the reality that before I could talk about emotional connections, I needed to connect to God as a child of God; through Him I needed to find myself and to embrace every blessed emotion created within me.

I look back on pictures of myself as a young woman and my heart aches. Photos capture the outward smile and mask the sadness within.

I absolutely hated myself: I hated my looks, I hated my height and weight, I hated my unrelenting need to please, need to accomplish, need to be the best. I was never satisfied. I couldn't accept doing my best; I had to be the best, standards that were impossible to meet and precursors to years of disappointment and frustration, a reel of memories that would play on a continuous loop in my head and hang heavy over my heart.

My eating disorder turned into a forty-year fight with God. It became the manifestation of my refusal to submit to Him and His will for me in my life. Decade after decade I was determined to do it my way, refusing to accept His love and guidance. I truly believed I knew best. My prayers were misguided, token attempts at a relationship; they were Christian posturing at its worst. So often I would tell myself, this isn't a life-threatening condition, it's just fifty-six pounds, but I was very much mistaken. My refusal to accept God's love and guidance was destroying me physically, emotionally, and spiritually. Unable to "delight in God's will and walk in His ways," as we beseech Him in that Sunday morning confession, I was back in the pew burdened by the pounds of sin, allowing God's gift of grace to become overshadowed by my looming silhouette and His words of absolution to be drowned out by the din of sins past.

Gentleness can define a "good" birth or family. Having been baptized into His family, God has gently and not so gently reminded me that I, too, have been born into a good family, His family. I really am His own dear child. Today I want to shed pounds of pride and vanity. I want to set aside stubbornness and self-righteousness. I want to let go of shame and emotional baggage. I want to come out of the dark and into the light. I want to radiate His love and grace. I want to find myself delighting in the fruit of His Holy Spirit as it grows and becomes the strong, gentle fruit of my own spirit.

Today I just want is to be four dress sizes smaller. There is nothing remotely righteous about my goal to be thinner, but I can't help remembering what God was able to do with the questionable hopes and dreams of my youth. Left to my own devices, I will continue to eat through pain and frustration. The increase in my weight will bring another layer of failure. I'll push God aside one minute and search frantically for Him the next. I'll rail at God in frustration and disappointment one day and then search for His answer in a quick and easy solution the next. But remembering that God's already got me by the hand, I'm hoping—no, I'm praying—that I will finally allow Him to lead. His forgiveness has been there all along, not as a magical transformation, but as a divine recreation. Through Him, I am renewed, restored, and revived to new life. I've been given another day, another chance.

And when I see a picture of myself, I pray that my heart might sing, knowing both an inner and outer beauty has been captured in the flash of a moment. For fifty-six years I've been content to leave memories in their old frames. I've settled for the consolation prize of life's challenges, denying myself "the peace that surpasses all understanding" (Philippians 4:7). My struggles with food aren't over. I only know that God has promised to be with me wherever I may go, wherever I may be. I also know that I've been the recipient of more than I deserve and dare hope for. I've been given His unmerited love and promised complete forgiveness.

And so I pray:

Lord Jesus, teach me to be generous.
Teach me to serve You as You deserve,
> *to give and not to count the cost, to fight and not to heed the wounds,*
> *to toil and not to seek for rest, to labor and not to seek reward,*
> *save that of knowing that I do Your will.*

> —St. Ignatius of Loyola

With God it can be so.

I Know That My Redeemer Lives

Words by Samuel Medley
Music arranged by John C. Hatton

I know that my Redeemer lives;
What comfort this sweet sentence gives!
He lives, He lives, who once was dead;
He lives, my everliving head.

He lives to bless me with His love;
He lives to plead for me above;
He lives my hungry soul to feed;
He lives to help in time of need.

He lives to grant me rich supply;
He lives to guide me with His eye;
He lives to comfort me when faint;
He lives to hear my soul's complaint.

He lives to silence all my fears;
He lives to wipe away my tears;
He lives to calm my troubled heart;
He lives all blessings to impart.

He lives, all glory to His name!
He lives, my Jesus, still the same;
Oh, the sweet joy this sentence gives;
I know that my Redeemer lives!

Faithfulness
Resting in a Relationship with God

Pistis

Greek for Faithfulness
Steadfast, unwavering

Chapter Nine

I DROVE TO THE MEMORIAL SERVICE not expecting to be bombarded with the intense range of emotions and flood of memories. My mother's brother was being remembered in the small town where they had grown up, the area where he had farmed the family's wheat fields. My own mom and dad had preceded him in death by ten years; Grandma and Grandpa had passed fifteen years before that. As I left home, my feelings were mixed: I dreaded the drive, hating the idea that I had lost a special member of the family, but I had to admit that I was looking forward to seeing everyone. There had been a small lull in gatherings, the quietness that can arise between the happier graduations and weddings of the younger generation and the sadder funerals and memorials for the older.

Driving by myself, I took roads not traveled in decades, and once I left the interstate, the long-forgotten sights and sounds came quickly. Grandma and Grandpa had lived in Eastern Washington. Grandpa emigrated from a farming region in northern Germany. Following an older brother, he settled and began farming wheat. He married a local girl and together they raised four children, their oldest girl (my mother), a son, and twin daughters. They were hardworking members of a proud, thriving little community.

Our family used to visit Grandma and Grandpa during the summer and at Christmas. Before the change in interstate speeds, the five-hour drive was closer to six hours, sometimes seven, if chains were required on the mountain pass. Our travels were constantly interrupted by backseat squabbles: "Mom, he's on my side." "Dad, can you tell her to quit looking at me?" Without the benefit of seatbelts, my brother and I could push the limits of my parents' patience, annoying each other for much of the drive. Fortunately we arrived to a houseful of cousins, separating us until the ride back home.

My first real summer job came between seventh and eighth grade when I helped my aunt during harvest. My aunt and uncle lived on a ranch about four miles from Grandma and Grandpa. My uncle was responsible for the farm, and extra help was always necessary during the two to three weeks needed to harvest the wheat. I helped cook and clean, an interesting job description as I look back, since I would grow up to do neither.

I take pride in the raising of my sons as future husbands. I don't cook or clean. Before planning for groceries, I budget for hair and facials, manicures and pedicures. The neighbor takes care of my landscaping needs. Kurt believes in the "happy wife/happy life" approach of smart husbands everywhere, keeping my car clean and running, and getting the shopping done. It didn't take Kyle and Kevin long to realize that their mother was different from many, that their nutritional livelihoods would depend on their ability to use the stove and negotiate the aisles of a grocery store, that they would need to know the location of a good dry cleaning service, and that a future career would need to pay the mortgage and much, much more. During the terrible market correction of 2008-2009, I had to confess to Kurt that he could survive the economic downtown and maintain his standard of living, if it weren't for his high maintenance wife. He thought it was a little joke.

As I drove along wheat fields on the final stretch of my trip, I looked across huge expanses of stubble glistening in the autumn sun. Little had changed in fifty years. That feeling of comfort and joy was abruptly shattered with my arrival in town. With time before the start of the memorial service, I took a little tour. The results were heartbreaking. Driving down Main Street, I was confronted with building after building, all empty, windows boarded up. The barrenness and desolation left me aching for the past. The hotel, drugstore, grocery store, bank, car dealership, gas station, and tavern were all distant memories. The once proud community was reduced to one church, a fertilizer store, and a grain elevator. New street signs led nowhere.

Determined to find some connection to treasured remembrances, I drove past my grandparents' home. The red geraniums in the window boxes were nowhere to be seen. The huge weeping willow was gone. Grandpa's shed had been replaced with a monstrous aluminum structure that could have housed his entire fleet of tractors, trucks, and combines. I'm sure Grandma's vegetable garden was buried under a layer of asphalt; I would never know, since a solid six-foot fence encircled the entire back lot.

Not wanting to risk feeling better, I took the entire tour a second time after the service and once again tried to capture a moment, a spot, a little piece of history to soothe my longing for yesterday. I struggled with the disconnect. The smell of the land, the sound of a chicken, the familiar turns on the way to the ranch, all transported me to another day in time, disguising the present. It was truly the end of an era.

I returned from the sadness of my weekend away to the frustrating task of transferring from an old computer to a new one. My high-tech life was changing yet again, this time leaving me with the grief and heartache of trying to get information from one machine to another as part of the twenty-first century's insatiable drive to be bigger—faster—stronger. Those around me had to suffer through tears and tirades as I upgraded and downloaded, a process that started out taking days and eventually lasted weeks. The only relief for my family was knowing that it would be another two years before they would have to endure the process all over again.

Living through the computer age, one of the great crossovers in human history, sounds conceptually like a phenomenal opportunity, a not-since-the-Gutenberg-printing-press experience, but I continually find myself peddling as fast as I can to keep up, always knowing just enough to be dangerous. Each day I am bombarded with new messages, more information, another program. I am connected 24/7. I am plugged in and linked up. I used to brush my teeth and say my prayers before bed. Now I check emails and MSN headlines.

Through it all, God has been the only constant. As life changed, as people came and went, as a small community quietly closed its doors, God's love and grace were unwavering, caring for all humankind while never losing sight of a young woman and her family. In a world of disposables, in a time when something's obsolete, if not new and improved, God remained faithful. To a girl who questioned and strayed and struggled and failed, God remained faithful.

At times I've been caught by feelings of loneliness. Loved by family, supported by friends, I still have moments when the quiet is unwelcome. Add to it the stress of chronic pain, times of separation, and a myriad of smaller and larger challenges that come with life on any particular day and the feelings of isolation can catch me unawares.

In Galatians, Paul puts faithfulness between goodness and gentleness in his list of fruit. As I reframed life in God's grace, I had to put faithfulness last, because it was the thread that held my life together at every moment, in every situation, throughout my youth and adulthood, as a daughter, wife, and mother.

In this day and age I have to be careful that I don't associate faithfulness with a fifteen-minute love connection on a cable reality show or the punch line to a bad joke on late night TV. I laugh—I cringe. I smirk—I moan. The excitement of tonight's adventure is drama for a scandal sheet's next cover page. I'm reminded of the silliness of it all until I see the cover of a news magazine highlighting the rising divorce rate. Like my mother before me, I now shake my head and wonder whatever happened to the good ol' days. It's easy to wonder if faithfulness has become an f-word, something not to be discussed over tea in polite society or a latte at the neighborhood coffee shop.

In our thirtieth year of marriage, the four of us have become the two of us as Kyle and Kevin make their own ways in the world. We are excited for the boys as we watch their lives unfold, but I still remember with longing our time together as a young family. As the boys left for college, the initial relief that came with having more and more time of my own got replaced with the agonizing thought, *What do I do now?* Missing soccer games during Kevin's first year in college, I asked Kurt to go to a friend's game. Kevin was astounded, "Mom, when I was playing all you did was complain about the cold."

Life has truly changed with each passing season, along with the people, places, and things that surround me. The one and only constant has been my Father in heaven, my Lord and Savior, and His Holy Spirit.

> When I needed His love,
>> when I needed His guidance,
>> when I needed His peace,
>> when I needed joy,
>>> and kindness,
>>> and goodness,
>> when I needed patience and gentleness,
>>> God was faithful.

When I was a ditzy teenager,
   when I was a defiant child,
   when I was looking for refuge from the storm,
   when I needed to be able to make music again,
     to forgive,
      and to grow as His child in order to mother His children,
   when I needed relief from pain,
   when I needed to find love for a beautiful woman specially
   chosen to do His work,
     God was faithful.

In truthfulness I struggle to find words with which to describe God's faithfulness, a faithfulness that extends from a love that is beyond measure, an indescribable, indefinable, inexplicable love that has encircled me without fail, without hesitation, unconditionally through joyous, sad, cringe-worthy, heartwarming, forgettable, and memorable moments in my life. To know that the very thought of me brings a smile to God's face brings me to my knees.

And then I'm able to arise in His light and stand tall in His love and grace. Through His faithfulness, I am filled with His Holy Spirit and the spirit of faithfulness.

I pray:

May the will of God, the Father, the Son and the Holy Spirit be done! Amen.

–*Martin Luther*

A Mighty Fortress Is Our God
Words and Music by Martin Luther

A might fortress is our God, a bulwark never failing;
Our helper He amid the flood of mortal ills prevailing:
For still our ancient foe doth seek to work us woe;
His craft and power are great, and, armed with cruel hate,
On earth is not his equal.

Did we in our own strength confide our striving would be losing;
Were not the right Man on our side, the Man of God's own choosing.
Dost ask who that may be? Christ Jesus, it is He;
Lord Sabaoth, His Name, from age to age the same,
And He must win the battle.

And though this world, with devils filled, should threaten to undo us;
We will not fear, for God hath willed His truth to triumph through us:
The Prince of Darkness grim, we tremble not for him;
His rage we can endure, for lo! his doom is sure,
One little word shall fell him.

That word above all earthly powers, no thanks to them abideth;
The Spirit and the gifts are ours through Him Who with us sideth:
Let goods and kindred go, this mortal life also;
The body they may kill: God's truth abideth still,
His kingdom is forever.

Afterword
Living Life in God's Grace

Afterword

URING THE HEALTHCARE DEBATE in Washington D.C., an outspoken cable commentator essentially summed up the discussion in two words: death and life. At the heart of the issue was death: preventing it, fighting it, resisting it, grabbing hold of anything and everything to forestall and postpone it, even though we know that it will ultimately overcome us—always has, always will. He went on to speak of our human will to live, to do whatever is necessary to extend life for another year or month or second. In his introduction he said the issue wasn't about preexisting conditions or the cost of insurance or other faults with the system; it was just about death on the one hand and life on the other.

The commentator's secular argument actually missed the spiritual truth: We do have a preexisting condition, a painful, chronic condition with no treatment and no cure—sin. With sin, our fate was sealed, and now we desperately try to grab hold of anything with the promise of life—more life, better life, easier life. Sadly our disobedience, our need for better, our insatiable desire for more got the best of us. We ate of the fruit that we had been told not to touch. The serpent promised the knowledge of good and evil. He was right. Eating the fruit, we learned that our refusal to obey our Creator would separate us from Good and leave us mired in the Evil of sin. Our separation from God was total and irreparable. It was a separation that left all of humankind in pain and misery, doing any- and everything to fill the void.

I was no different. My own separation from God left me in terrible pain, physically, emotionally, and spiritually. I sought to end the suffering in my own way, in my own time. I failed miserably. There was no way to repair the irreparable. My missteps and refusal to acknowledge my own failings pushed me further and further away from God's promised redemption. Ultimately I knew that it would be divine intervention that would finally restore my relationship with my heavenly Father, that the death and resurrection of His Son would finally provide the peace I wanted so dearly; I just needed to get an ego the size of Mount Sinai out of the way.

So back to my original question: Now what?

Not long ago I was part of a wonderful weekend at church in which we talked about living life as God's people. The opening session began with a story about the speaker's chance encounter with a well-known musical conductor on a flight from San Francisco to Chicago. The gentleman asked our speaker, a pastor, "What is your business?" He launched into a long list of activities surrounding his work for the church, a list that ultimately impressed even him. The conductor just listened and smiled, so the pastor responded by asking him, "What do you do?" At this point the conductor clarified the difference between his question, "What is your business?" and the pastor's question, "What do you do?" by saying, "My business is to bring people to Christ. To do that, I'm a musical conductor." After forty years in the ministry, the pastor was floored. He had never had his call to God's service explained so clearly, nor life's priorities so plainly identified. The conductor got out his Bible and suggested they study together during the remainder of the flight. The pastor sheepishly responded that he was without a Bible, so the conductor grabbed a second copy from his carry-on.

I remember very little else from our three days together. Like the pastor, I, too, was stunned by the question, What is my business? For the young woman who was uncertain about her place in God's family and His place in hers, for the older woman who was still confused, questions regarding identity were suddenly moot:

> My business is to bring others to Christ.
> To do that, I'm a wife and a mother.
> My business is to bring others to Christ.
> To do that, I help manage a financial planning practice.
> My business is to bring others to Christ.
> To do that, I live in Monroe.
> My business is to bring others to Christ.

To do that, I grab a latte every morning,
I get my nails done every Tuesday,
and I play my violin during worship.
My business is to bring others to Christ.
To do that, I write.

In an age of terror alerts, "lead with bleed" newscasts, and financial corrections, recessions, and depressions, I get to share the hope and promise given to me as a follower of Christ. From a place of imperfection, I get to share the perfect love of God for His people. At any given moment on any given day, my role as God's child is to bring others to Him, to share the enormity of His love with the lost, the disillusioned, the overworked, and the hungry, to speak of God's forgiveness with those I know and with those God puts before me. My shortcomings and failings are the very tools He needs for the work ahead. God has chosen me to be a witness to the life that's possible in Him and through Him. Whether I'm standing at the grocery store (not likely) or getting a facial (more likely), I get to be His representative at that exact moment. Some will never see the inside of a church, but they'll see me. Some may never hold a Bible, but they'll read volumes in my face.

The responsibilities are more than a little daunting. After fifty-six years, it's impossible to deny I've had more than a few regrettable, forgettable moments, not exactly the finest witness to God's greatest gift of love and forgiveness. Some of life's foibles are cute, but stripped of the humor, they're really recollections of a life lived in sin. There have actually been many moments better suited for some kind of a witness protection program, not for my own safety, but for the well-being of the community at large. And then I stop and remember that my business is to bring others to Christ. To do that, I am my own loving, imperfect, dynamic, challenging, passionate, impatient self, just the person God chose.

Ironically Paul speaks of fruit in his letter to the people of Galatia. Remembering that it was the fruit of disobedience and sin that actually separated us from God, I smile thinking of a most remarkable God who would repair the relationship with His children by sharing—freely—the fruit of love, joy, peace, patience, kindness, goodness, faithfulness, gentleness, and self-control. "Against such there is no law" (Galatians 5:23).

After His transfiguration, Jesus left the mountain with His disciples. He needed to finish his ministry among the people. There was still much to do. There is still much to do. My business is to bring others to Christ. To do that I will live each day in love, joy, peace, patience, kindness, goodness, faithfulness, gentleness, and self-control. So help me, God!

> *Therefore, since we have been justified through faith, we have peace with God through our Lord Jesus Christ, through whom we have gained access by faith into this grace in which we now stand. And we rejoice in the hope of the glory of God. Not only so, but we also rejoice in our sufferings, because we know that suffering produces perseverance; perseverance, character; and character, hope. And hope does not disappoint us, because God has poured out his love into our hearts by the Holy Spirit, whom he has given us.*
>
> *—Romans 5:1-5*

I pray:

> *May the grace of our Lord Jesus Christ, and the love of God, and the fellowship of the Holy Spirit be with us all, now and forever more. Amen.*
>
> *—2 Corinthians 13:14*

With God it can be so!

Beautiful Savior

Words from the Munsterisch Gesangbuch, translated by Joseph A. Seiss
Music from a Silesian folk tune

Beautiful Savior, King of creation,
Son of God and Son of Man!
Truly I'd love Thee, Truly I'd serve Thee,
Light of my soul, my joy, my crown.

Fair are the meadows, Fair are the woodlands,
Robed in flow'rs of blooming spring;
Jesus is fairer, Jesus is purer,
He makes our sorr'wing spirit sing.

Fair is the sunshine, Fair is the moonlight,
Bright the sparkling stars on high;
Jesus shines brighter, Jesus shines purer
Than all the angels in the sky.

Beautiful Savior, Lord of the nations,
Son of God and Son of Man!
Glory and honor, Praise, adoration
Now and forevermore by Thine!

Give the Gift of
Fruit of My Spirit

Reframing Life in God's Grace to Your Friends and Colleagues
**Check your leading bookstore, Amazon.com,
or order here for only $12.95 plus tax and shipping!**

☐ YES, I want _____ copies of *Fruit of My Spirit*

☐ *Books x $12.95 per book* $_____
Washington Residents add 8.6% Sales Tax $_____
$3.00 shipping per book $_____
TOTAL $_____

Allow 15 days for delivery.
Please make checks payable to **Rhododendron Books**.
Canadian orders must be accompanied by a postal money order in U.S. funds.

If you'd like to pay with a credit card, please go to Amazon.com

☐ Yes, I am interested in having Deanna Nowadnick speak to my company, association, school, or organization. Please send my order or information to:

Name _____
Organization _____
Address _____
City/State/Zip _____
Phone _____
Email _____

Return this form to:
Rhododendron Books • P.O. Box 1586 • Monroe, WA 98272
You may also fax this form to (866) 743-4089
www.rhododendronbooks.com • www.fruitofmyspirit.com

CPSIA information can be obtained at www.ICGtesting.com
Printed in the USA
BVOW030018061211

277643BV00007B/5/P